CONTROVERSIES IN PSYCHOLOGY

Longman Essential Psychology
Series editor: Andrew M. Colman

CONTROVERSIES IN PSYCHOLOGY

EDITED BY

Andrew M. Colman

LONGMAN
London and New York

Addison Wesley Longman Limited
Edinburgh Gate
Harlow
Essex CM20 2JE, England
and Associated Companies throughout the world.

*Published in the United States of America
by Longman Publishing, New York*

© 1994 Routledge
This edition © 1995 Longman Group Limited
Compilation © 1995 Andrew Colman

This edition first published 1995
Second impression 1996

ISBN 0 582 27803 1 PPR

British Library Cataloguing-in-Publication Data
A catalogue record for this book is available from the British Library.

Library of Congress Cataloging-in-Publication Data
A catalogue record for this book is available from the Library of Congress.

Typeset by 25 in 10/12pt Times
Produced through Longman Malaysia, GPS

CONTENTS

NOTES ON EDITORS AND CONTRIBUTORS

SUSAN BLACKMORE studied psychology and physiology at St Hilda's College, Oxford, took her doctorate in parapsychology at the University of Surrey and then worked at Bristol and Bath Universities and as a writer and broadcaster. She is Senior Lecturer in Psychology at the University of the West of England at Bristol. Her current research interests are the origins of belief in the paranormal and near-death experiences. She is the author of *Beyond the Body: An Investigation of Out-of-the-Body Experiences* (1982), *The Adventures of a Parapsychologist* (1986), and *Dying to Live: Science and the Near-Death Experience* (1993).

ANDREW M. COLMAN is Reader in Psychology at the University of Leicester, having previously taught at Rhodes and Cape Town Universities in South Africa. He is the founder and former editor of the journal *Current Psychology* and Chief Examiner for the British Psychological Society's Qualifying Examination. His books include *Facts, Fallacies and Frauds in Psychology* (1987), *What is Psychology? The Inside Story* (2nd edn, 1988), and *Game Theory and its Applications in the Social and Biological Sciences* (2nd edn, 1995).

MARY CRAWFORD is Professor of Psychology and Graduate Director of Women's Studies at the University of South Carolina. She received her PhD in experimental psychology from the University of Delaware. She is active in the Division on the Psychology of Women of the American Psychological Association and in many organizations concerned with gender equity and feminist scholarship. She is Book Review Editor for *Psychology of Women Quarterly*, a member of the international editorial advisory board of *Feminism and Psychology*, and Research Director for the Women's College Coalition. She is a fellow of the American Psychological Association and the American Psychological Society. Her publications include the book (co-edited with M. Gentry) *Gender and Thought: Psychological Perspectives* (1989).

ROBERT T. CROYLE is Associate Professor of Psychology at the University of Utah, Salt Lake City. He took his doctorate in psychology from Princeton University, New Jersey, and has taught at Williams College and the University of Washington. He has published articles on attitude change, judgement biases, and health-related memory, and is co-editor (with J. A. Skelton) of *Mental Representation in Health and Illness* (1991).

ELIZABETH F. LOFTUS is Professor of Psychology and Adjunct Professor of Law at the University of Washington, Seattle. She took her doctorate in psychology at Stanford University, California. She is the author of 16 books, including *Eyewitness Testimony* (1979) and co-author (with K. Ketchman) of *Witness for the Defense* (1991).

RHODA K. UNGER is Professor of Psychology and Director of the Honors Program at Montclair State College in New Jersey. She received her PhD in experimental psychology from Harvard University, and was the first recipient of the Carolyn Wood Sherif Award from the Division on the Psychology of Women of the American Psychological Association. She is also the recipient of two Distinguished Publication Awards from the Association for Women in Psychology. She is active in various feminist organizations within psychology and has lectured extensively in the United States and abroad. She has published six books; she is the author of *Female and Male* (1979), co-editor (with V. E. O'Leary and B. S. Wallston) of *Women, Gender, and Social Psychology* (1985), and editor of *Representations: Social Constructions of Gender* (1989).

GRAHAM F. WAGSTAFF is Senior Lecturer in Psychology at the University of Liverpool. His main research and teaching interests are in social psychology and he has a particular interest in social psychological and forensic aspects of hypnosis. He is one of the founder members of the British Society of Experimental and Clinical Hypnosis. He has published widely in the area of hypnosis and is author of *Hypnosis, Compliance and Belief* (1981). He is currently writing a book on the psychology and philosophy of justice.

JOHN WEINMAN is Professor of Psychology as Applied to Medicine at the United Medical and Dental Schools of Guy's and St Thomas' Hospital in the University of London. He first trained in clinical psychology at the Royal Free Hospital, London, and then obtained his doctorate at the Institute of Neurology after four years' full-time research with the Medical Research Council. He is the editor-in-chief of *Psychology and Health: An International Journal*. He is the author of *An Outline of Psychology as Applied to Medicine* (1987) and the editor of several other books on aspects of health psychology.

SERIES EDITOR'S PREFACE

The *Longman Essential Psychology* series comprises twelve concise and inexpensive paperback volumes covering all of the major topics studied in undergraduate psychology degree courses. The series is intended chiefly for students of psychology and other subjects with psychology components, including medicine, nursing, sociology, social work, and education. Each volume contains five or six accessibly written chapters by acknowledged authorities in their fields, and each chapter includes a list of references and a small number of recommendations for further reading.

Most of the material was prepared originally for the Routledge *Companion Encyclopedia of Psychology* but with a view to later paperback subdivision – the contributors were asked to keep future textbook readers at the front of their minds. Additional material has been added for the paperback series: new co-editors have been recruited for nine of the volumes that deal with highly specialized topics, and each volume has a new introduction, a glossary of technical terms including a number of entries written specially for this edition, and a comprehensive new index.

I am grateful to my literary agents Sheila Watson and Amanda Little for clearing a path through difficult terrain towards the publication of this series, to Sarah Caro of Longman for her patient and efficient preparation of the series, to Brian Parkinson, David Stretch, and Susan Dye for useful advice and comments, and to Carolyn Preston for helping with the compilation of the glossaries.

ANDREW M. COLMAN

INTRODUCTION

Andrew M. Colman
University of Leicester, England

This book deals with issues that arouse debate, argument, and controversy, not only within the psychological community but also in the public arena. In addition to being controversial, they are topics that students find especially intriguing, and they are therefore popular topics for seminars and discussion groups. Students and general readers alike seem to be attracted to books that focus on controversial issues. Controversies in psychology are not only interesting but also highly instructive, because they clearly expose the reasoning processes and research methodologies that lie behind the psychologists' conclusions. As the philosopher of science Karl Popper argued persuasively (see, for example, Popper, 1972), ideas that have withstood vigorous criticism are generally preferable to those that have been accepted uncritically or dogmatically, because the process of criticism exposes errors that can then be eliminated. It is worth adding that criticism also tends to cause the underlying ideas to be expressed more clearly and therefore to be better understood.

There is another significant property shared by the topics covered in this volume. They are all difficult to classify within the conventional course modules of the standard undergraduate curriculum, as represented by the titles of the other books in this series, namely *Cognitive Psychology*, *Developmental Psychology*, *Social Psychology*, and so on. In spite of the difficulty of classifying them, the topics discussed in the following chapters are all related to research problems of sufficient importance to have attracted sustained research, and they tend to be taught in degree courses under a variety of different headings, including 'Special Topics' and 'Options'.

In chapter 1, Susan Blackmore provides a critical survey of research into parapsychology. The word itself comes from the Greek *para*, which means beyond, prefixed to the word *psychology*. Parapsychology is a small but well established and active field of research devoted to the investigation of psychological phenomena that purport to be paranormal, or to use a more familiar word, supernatural. Blackmore traces the historical background of parapsychology (for a more detailed historical survey see Beloff, 1994) and then evaluates the scientific evidence regarding a number of possibly paranormal phenomena, including ESP (extra-sensory perception: perception without the use of normal sensory processes), PK (psychokinesis: the movement or change of physical objects by purely mental processes), psychic experiences, out-of-body experiences, and survival after death.

It is only through properly controlled scientific investigations that the reality of such phenomena can be established convincingly. There is an abundance of non-scientific, anecdotal evidence for spontaneous paranormal phenomena, or psi phenomena as they are often inelegantly called (from the Greek letter *psi*, representing *psyche*, soul, and *psychical*, spiritual). We have all heard accounts of psi experiences from relatives, friends, and acquaintances, and early psychical research was devoted largely to collecting and examining just such accounts as these. But anecdotal evidence of this kind relies on the testimony of those who report it, and more than two centuries ago the Scottish philosopher David Hume (1748/1902, section 10) put forward a decisive argument against accepting such reports. He pointed out that an anecdotal report of an allegedly paranormal event (or of anything else, for that matter) always entails exactly three logical possibilities: either the report is true, or it is false because the informant is mistaken, or it is false because the informant is lying. Now if an informant reports something that is supposed to be true but is intrinsically unlikely, then the crucial question is whether one of the alternatives, namely that the informant is mistaken or lying, is even less likely. The answer always has to be no: a paranormal event must have violated a law of nature and must therefore be as unlikely as anything could be, because if it did not violate any law of nature, then the claim that it was paranormal would collapse. It follows from this that the likelihood that the informant is mistaken or lying must be greater, because that would not violate any law of nature. Consequently, there are never good grounds for believing merely anecdotal accounts of paranormal phenomena. Perhaps surprisingly, Hume's argument also applies, with minor modifications, to a belief that one has experienced a paranormal event at first hand, because even the testimony of one's own senses can be mistaken without violating any law of nature (Mackie, 1982, ch. 1). Because anecdotal evidence is unpersuasive, paranormal phenomena must be investigated through properly controlled scientific experiments of the type discussed by Blackmore in chapter 1.

In chapter 2, Graham F. Wagstaff discusses hypnosis and the controversy surrounding the interpretation of various strange phenomena associated with it. The controversy over credulous versus sceptical interpretations of hypnotic phenomena, as they have come to be called, can be traced to France in 1784. The King of France at that time appointed a scientific commission to investigate the practice of animal magnetism by the Viennese physician Franz Anton Mesmer. The controversy over the interpretation of hypnotic phenomena is perhaps the longest-running debate in the whole history of psychology. Hypnosis never fully recovered from the debunking of Mesmer's theories, although the phenomena of hypnosis really have nothing to do with animal magnetism or with Mesmer's curative methods. Hypnosis's reputation in the popular imagination was further damaged by George Du Maurier's influential novel, *Trilby*, which was published in 1894 and made into a popular film by Archie Mayo in 1931. The story is about a young model called Trilby O'Farral, groomed as a singer by a sinister and overbearing hypnotist called Svengali, who exerts almost supernatural powers over her and deprives her of all ability to think and act for herself. Wagstaff's chapter shows that this image of hypnosis could hardly be further from the truth. Although a great deal is now known about hypnosis, the debate over its interpretation remains tantalizingly unresolved.

Wagstaff deals critically with the debate about whether or not hypnosis is (or entails) an altered state of consciousness. He then goes on to discuss the physiology of hypnosis, its apparently transcendent properties, and its major phenomena, including trance logic (the peculiar willingness of hypnotized subjects to tolerate certain kinds of logical inconsistencies), hypnotic amnesia, hypnotic analgesia, and hypnotic susceptibility. He concludes with a brief discussion of clinical applications of hypnosis and susceptibility to hypnosis. According to the sceptical interpretation, with which Wagstaff is generally sympathetic, all hypnotic phenomena can be explained without assuming any special state of consciousness. The phenomenon of hypnotic analgesia presents perhaps the most severe challenge to this interpretation, but Wagstaff argues that even the established ability of susceptible hypnotic subjects to undergo major surgery without anaesthetics can be explained without invoking any special hypnotic state. For a more detailed (and more credulous) account of hypnotic analgesia, see Hilgard and Hilgard (1994). Hypnosis has occasionally been applied in an attempt to obtain more or better evidence from witnesses in criminal trials; research in that area is discussed in chapter 4 in connection with psychology and the law.

Chapter 3, by Mary Crawford and Rhoda K. Unger, contains a detailed survey of various lines of research related to gender issues in psychology. This has been an active field of psychological research and debate since the emergence of feminist thinking in psychology during the 1970s. Many contemporary authorities in this field, including the authors of this chapter, draw a distinction between sex differences and gender differences. According to this view, sex differences are the genetically determined biological differences between male and female, whereas gender differences are the differences arising from psychological, social, and cultural influences acting on biological sex differences. This chapter first examines a number of conceptual and methodological issues surrounding gender-related research. It then focuses on gender and development throughout the lifespan, what the authors call "doing gender" (the way in which people's preconceptions based on sex differences affect gender-characteristic patterns of interpersonal interaction, such as self-presentational strategies and interactions between people of different status), and finally sexuality and relationships in the sociocultural context. More extended discussions of gender issues in psychology can be found in the further reading recommended by Crawford and Unger and in Doyle and Paludi's (1995) book, *Sex and Gender: The Human Experience*.

In chapter 4, Robert T. Croyle and Elizabeth F. Loftus survey all major aspects of psychology and the law. Most of the research in this area has concentrated on aspects of criminal trials, especially factors affecting the validity of eyewitness testimony and psychological processes in jury decision making. However, a considerable amount of research attention has also been paid to psychological aspects of sentencing and general treatment of convicted criminals. Croyle and Loftus's chapter provides a review of research in these and other fields of investigation broadly related to psychology and the law. As might be expected, many aspects of psychology and the law are highly controversial. For readers who wish to delve further into these issues, the *Handbook of Psychology in Legal Contexts* (1995) and the books by Bartol and Bartol (1994) and Wrightsman, Nietzel and Fortune (1994) may be useful, in addition to Croyle and Loftus's suggested further reading.

The last chapter in this volume is chapter 5, by John Weinman, on health psychology. This area of research relates to psychological factors in the promotion and maintenance of health, the prevention and treatment of illness, and the identification of psychological causes and correlates of all forms of health and illness. Chapter 5 covers various aspects of research in health psychology, including the controversial relationship between stress and health, the effects of differing lifestyles on health, coping strategies and the role of social support among people suffering from chronic illnesses, psychological responses to medical investigations and treatments, and, at a more theoretical level, various explanations that have been put forward to explain health-related behaviour. Further information on these and other issues in health psychology is contained in Weinman's suggested further reading and in the books by Stroebe and Stroebe (1995) and Taylor (1995).

Gender differences in health and illness have been reliably established, although neither chapter 5 (on health psychology) nor chapter 3 (on gender issues in psychology) discuss them in any detail. As an example, the evidence is overwhelming that in western industrial societies – and perhaps in others as well – women are significantly more prone to depression than men. Research evidence suggests that this may be due to gender differences in coping styles. In a detailed review of gender differences in depression,

Nolen-Hoeksema (1987) concluded that regardless of whether the depression is biological, psychological, or social in origin, women tend to ruminate significantly more than men – in other words, they tend to spend more time mulling over their problems. In contrast, men tend to distract themselves more than women do, which may in some circumstances be a more effective strategy for coping with depression. This line of research suggests that gender differences in depression, and perhaps in other mental disorders as well, may be due to differences between the coping styles and strategies of men and women.

In spite of the compact size of this volume, the range of subject matter contained within it is wide and varied. Readers who wish to pursue any of the topics in depth are strongly urged to follow the suggestions for further reading at the end of each chapter and perhaps also the additional suggestions contained in this introduction.

REFERENCES

Bartol, C. R., & Bartol, A. M. (1994). *Psychology and the law: Research and application* (2nd edn). Pacific Grove, CA: Brooks/Cole.

Beloff, J. (1994). *Parapsychology: A concise history*. New York: St Martin's Press.

Doyle, J. A., & Paludi, M. A. (1995). *Sex and gender: The human experience* (3rd edn). Madison, WI: Brown & Benchmark.

Handbook of psychology in legal contexts (1995). New York: Wiley.

Hilgard, E. R., & Hilgard, J. R. (1994). *Hypnosis in the relief of pain* (revised edition), New York: Brunner/Mazel.

Hume, D. (1902). *Enquiry concerning human understanding*, (edited by L. A. Selby-Bigge). Oxford: Oxford University Press. (Original work published 1748.)

Mackie, J. L. (1982). *The miracle of theism: Arguments for and against the existence of god*. Oxford: Clarendon.

Nolen-Hoeksema, S. (1987). Sex differences in unipolar depression: Evidence and theory. *Psychological Bulletin, 101*, 259–82.

Popper, K. R. (1972). *Conjectures and refutations: The growth of scientific knowledge* (4th edn). London: Routledge & Kegan Paul.

Stroebe, W., & Stroebe, M. S. (1995). *Social psychology and health*. Pacific Grove, CA: Brooks/Cole.

Taylor, S. (1995). *Health psychology* (3rd edn). New York: McGraw-Hill.

Wrightsman, L. S., Nietzel, M. T., & Fortune, W. H. (1994). *Psychology and the legal system* (3rd edn). Pacific Grove, CA: Brooks/Cole.

1

PARAPSYCHOLOGY

Susan Blackmore
University of the West of England, Bristol, England

Psychical research and	**Psychic experiences**
spiritualism	**Spontaneous cases**
The founding of	**Out-of-body experiences**
parapsychology	**Survival of death**
The development of	**Criticism and scepticism**
parapsychology	**Further reading**
Free-response ESP research	**References**
PK and random events	

Parapsychology has been a controversial science since its inception, with experimenters claiming results that cannot be explained by chance and critics arguing that the best explanations are methodological flaws, statistical errors, or outright fraud. Methods have gradually improved, but the goal of a conclusively convincing demonstration or a repeatable experiment has not been achieved. Fully automated experiments have provided new evidence, and meta-analyses have revealed consistent features in whole areas of research.

PSYCHICAL RESEARCH AND SPIRITUALISM

The origins of parapsychology are often traced back to the start of spiritualism, a Christian faith with the added dimension of spirit communication through mediumship. Kate and Margaretta Fox are usually credited with being the first mediums. As children in 1848 in the little New York town of Hydesville, they heard raps and banging apparently from the spirit of a man buried beneath their wooden house. Neighbours and visitors wanted to communicate with the spirits themselves and soon the Fox sisters began giving public demonstrations.

From the start there was controversy, with some investigators arguing that the girls were clicking their joints to produce the noises. In a dramatic public confession in 1888 they demonstrated just this and said they had been cheating all along, but later they retracted. Critics accept the confessions as the end of the matter while supporters argue that the sisters were by then penniless and alcoholic and were bribed to confess (Brandon, 1983; Podmore, 1902).

By this time thousands of mediums were practising across Europe and the USA. Spirits were heard speaking through floating trumpets, cold breezes and touches were felt, music mysteriously played, and "ectoplasm", a substance supposedly exuded from the bodies of certain mediums, "materialized" in the form of spirits. In "table tipping", sitters placed their hands on a table's surface and the spirits answered their questions by tipping the table up or banging its legs on the floor. In one of the first experimental studies, the physicist Michael Faraday (1791–1867) tried to determine where the force came from. He stuck pieces of card to the table, under the sitters' fingers, and showed that they slipped along in the direction of the table's movement. It was not the table (pulled by the spirits) but the sitters' hands that moved first. He suggested that the sitters were not frauds but used "unconscious muscular action" (Faraday, 1853).

For him this was the end of the matter, but mediumship continued to grow. Among many famous mediums was Eusapia Palladino, who began her mediumistic career as an orphan in Naples and apparently levitated, materialized extra limbs, caused inexplicable noises, and made furniture glide about. In 1895 she was caught cheating, but some researchers were convinced that she had produced genuine phenomena under controlled conditions (Gauld, 1968). Mediums could readily purchase equipment for augmenting their acts, such as muslin drapes, luminous paint, slates on which spirits could mysteriously reply to questions, and trumpets which could float around unaided in the dark. Whether any mediums operated entirely without such aids has never been resolved. Some argue that any medium who is caught cheating once must be presumed always to be cheating, while others argue that the pressures on even the best of mediums mean that they may resort to fraud in exceptional circumstances. This issue still appears in the arguments about special subjects such as Uri Geller (Randi, 1975).

It is often claimed that one medium, Daniel Dunglas Home (pronounced Hume), was never caught cheating. He worked in reasonably well-lit rooms, unlike many mediums who preferred total darkness. He apparently handled live coals without burning, materialized glowing hands, levitated heavy tables, and even floated out of one window and into the next (Gauld, 1968). The famous chemist, Sir William Crookes, was convinced that his powers implied a new form of energy (Gauld, 1968; Grattan-Guinness, 1982).

2

Of course, if claims like these were genuine they would present a direct challenge to science. In this late Victorian era physics was enormously successful and Darwinism had come as a threat to many people's beliefs. Evolution in particular and the materialist view in general were strongly opposed by the Church, and some saw spiritualism as providing the evidence they needed to refute them. If the spirits of the dead could appear and speak, then materialism was false. Scientists and scholars began to take the claims seriously and to investigate them. It was in this context that, in 1882, the Society for Psychical Research (SPR) was founded in London.

Among its founder members were Edmund Gurney, Frederick Myers, and Henry Sidgwick, Fellow of Trinity College, Cambridge, and the SPR's first president. They established their objectives, now enshrined in every issue of the *Journal of the Society for Psychical Research*, as "to examine without prejudice or prepossession and in a scientific spirit those faculties of man, real or supposed, which appear to be inexplicable on any generally recognized hypothesis". They established committees to study thought transference, mesmerism, apparitions and haunted houses, and physical phenomena of mediumship.

One of their major motivations was to determine whether there is life after death, or survival. In an enormous project, the "Census of Hallucinations", 17,000 people were asked whether they had ever seen or felt something, or heard a voice, that was not due to any physical cause. Among the recognizable hallucinations of people, far more than could be expected occurred within twelve hours either way of that person's death. It seemed to be evidence for apparitions of the dying. Thousands of accounts of spontaneous experiences were collected and published, including telepathy, psychic dreams, apparitions, and collective hallucinations (Gurney, Myers, & Podmore, 1886).

The problems of drawing conclusions from spontaneous cases were obvious, and many preferred to carry out experiments. The first experiments into thought transference, or telepathy as it became known after 1882 (Grattan-Guinness, 1982), used what would now be called "free-response" methods. For example, the percipient or receiver tried to draw the picture the agent or sender was looking at. Although many striking hits were obtained, it is difficult to assess how many would be expected by chance. However, even in the 1880s statistical methods for estimating probabilities of guessing at playing cards or numbers were being developed, though the first large-scale experiments of this kind were probably those carried out in 1912 by John Coover (1917). This laid the foundation on which parapsychology was to be built.

THE FOUNDING OF PARAPSYCHOLOGY

Two people were almost entirely responsible for the founding of parapsychology in the 1930s – J. B. Rhine and his wife Louisa (Mauskopf & McVaugh, 1980). Trained as biologists they, like the psychical researchers before them, wanted to find evidence against a purely materialist view of human nature. Indeed the laboratory which now continues the work they began at Duke University in Durham, North Carolina, is called the Foundation for Research on the Nature of Man. Although their aims were the same, they wanted to get right away from any associations with spiritualism and bring their new science firmly into the laboratory. They renamed it parapsychology, began to develop experimental methods, and defined their terms operationally. Throughout their long research careers J. B. Rhine concentrated more on the experimental methods and Louisa Rhine on the collection of spontaneous cases (L. E. Rhine, 1981). He preferred to tackle the problem of verification by using statistical and experimental techniques; she preferred to collect large numbers of cases, hoping that they would teach us something about the nature of psychic phenomena even if many could never be verified.

In 1934 J. B. Rhine's first book launched the term "extrasensory perception" (ESP). This was a general term used to cover three types of communication supposedly occurring without the use of the senses: telepathy, in which the information comes from another person; clairvoyance, in which it comes from distant objects or events; and precognition, in which the information comes from the future (see Figure 1).

In the early telepathy experiments a receiver or percipient had to guess the identity of a target being looked at by an agent or sender. To make the task as easy as possible, a set of simple symbols was developed and made into cards called Zener cards (after their designer) or ESP cards. They consisted of a circle, square, cross, star, and wavy lines – 5 of each in a pack of 25 cards (see Figure 2). The order of the cards was determined initially by shuffling and later by the use of random number tables or other methods. It is extremely important for targets in ESP experiments to be properly

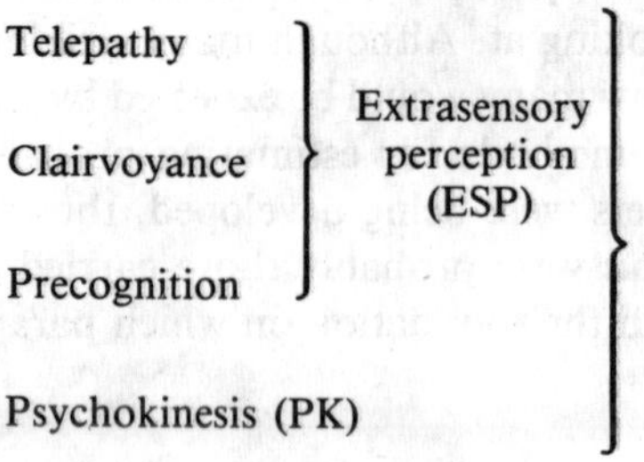

```
Telepathy      ⎫
               ⎬  Extrasensory
Clairvoyance   ⎭  perception      ⎫
                  (ESP)           ⎬ PSI
Precognition   ⎱                  ⎪
                                  ⎭
Psychokinesis (PK)
```

Figure 1 The four types of psi

4

Figure 2 The five symbols on traditional Zener cards. A pack consists of 25 cards, five of each symbol. They were designed to be simple and easy to distinguish but are tedious to use

randomized so that the results cannot be affected by systematic biases of any kind. Shuffling is not an adequate method.

In clairvoyance experiments the pack was randomized out of sight of anyone, and in precognition experiments its order was decided only *after* the guesses had been made. To obtain significant results, even with a very weak ESP effect, long series of guesses were made. The technique appeared to be successful, and the Rhines reported results that were far beyond what could be expected by chance.

Also in 1934 they began another controversial step, research into psychokinesis (PK). Many of their subjects claimed to be able to affect things at a distance by the power of the mind, and a gambler suggested they might test whether he could influence the roll of dice. Rhine subsequently turned this into an experimental method, first using hand-thrown dice and then a dice-throwing machine. The results were not as impressive as the ESP results but nevertheless seemed to suggest some paranormal ability, or "psi" power (J. B. Rhine, 1947). The term "psi" came to be used as a general term to cover any paranormal phenomena or the hypothesized mechanism underlying them. It includes both ESP and PK (see Figure 1).

The development of these definitions was an important step, but the definitions themselves are problematic (Alcock, 1981). All are negative in the sense that they depend on ruling out "normal" communication before the paranormal can be assumed. Progress in parapsychology's experimental methods has necessarily been designed to exclude the "normal" ever more securely. However, this inevitably leaves it open for critics to argue for ever more devious ways in which sensory communication or outright fraud might occur. Another consequence of some definitions is that the field of parapsychology is ever-shrinking. For example, hypnosis used to be considered part of psychical research, as did hallucinations and lucid dreams, until psychologists made progress in understanding them. As the psychologist Edwin Boring (1966) put it, a scientific success is a failure for psychical research. This is inevitable if parapsychology is defined as the study of the paranormal (e.g., Thalbourne, 1982) and this may be one reason why some parapsychologists now prefer to define their subject matter in terms of psychic *experiences*, without commitment to a particular explanation (e.g., Broughton, 1991).

THE DEVELOPMENT OF PARAPSYCHOLOGY

The controversy provoked by the Rhines spread around the world. Early problems in methodology and experimental design were detected, such as being able to read the symbols from the back of the cards, inadequate shuffling of the cards, biased dice, incomplete separation of the subjects, or the possibility of recording errors. When these were ironed out, some significant results continued. Their statistics were also criticized until in 1937 the President of the American Institute of Mathematical Statistics declared that if the experiments were properly performed, the statistical analysis was essentially valid (J. B. Rhine, 1947). Soon others, appreciating the importance of these findings, if they were true, tried to replicate them.

Among these was S. G. Soal, a mathematician at Queen Mary College, London, who spent five unsuccessful years trying. Another researcher, Whateley Carington, had been successful using objects on his mantelpiece as targets and had found that sometimes his subjects guessed the object before or after the one they were supposed to be guessing, a phenomenon that later became known as the "displacement effect" (J. B. Rhine, 1969). Following Carington's suggestions, Soal checked for guessing targets ahead and behind. In the results of one subject, Basil Shackleton, he found significant scores and went on to use Shackleton in what became his most famous experiments.

The odds against the results he obtained occurring by chance were astronomical (Soal & Bateman, 1954). To ensure that Shackleton could not be cheating, rigid controls were employed and other scientists used as observers throughout. These experiments, along with Rhine's, became the mainstay of the evidence for ESP (West, 1954).

As so often happens with significant results, accusations of fraud abounded. One of Soal's agents claimed that she had seen Soal changing figures in the target list. This provoked a series of many re-analyses and investigations of Soal's work, none of which could conclusively incriminate or exonerate him. In 1978 Betty Markwick, a member of the Society for Psychical Research in London, hoped to clear Soal's name by using a computer to search through the voluminous log tables he claimed to have used to decide his targets. She failed to find them. Only a tedious hand search revealed some repeated sequences and then the odd discovery that some sequences had numbers added in. All of these corresponded to hits, and when they were removed the results fell to chance (Markwick, 1978). It had taken a quarter of a century to solve the mystery and prove that Soal had cheated, and in that time thousands of people had been convinced that this evidence for ESP was genuine. As in many other cases, finding out whether he had cheated required at least as much work as the original experiments.

Meanwhile, research in parapsychology continued. In addition to finding subjects who could score higher than chance expectation, some subjects scored significantly *below* chance expectation, that is, psi missing. A decline effect was also found, whereby results tended to decline from the start of an experiment or session, as though novelty or freshness was required for success. These "signs of psi" added to the evidence but still did not reveal much, if anything, about the new phenomena that supposedly had been found. Some researchers tired of simply seeking more and more evidence to convince the critics and wanted to find out more about psi itself, in what would now be called "process oriented" rather than "proof oriented" research.

One of the best known of the early findings was the "sheep–goat" effect. Gertrude Schmeidler divided subjects into believers, whom she called sheep, and disbelievers or goats. She found that sheep consistently scored higher than goats, who often psi-missed (Schmeidler & McConnell, 1958). A review of sheep–goat experiments many years later indicated that the effect is widespread across many experiments (Palmer, 1971) suggesting that belief or motivation might be important in psi ability.

If experimenters needed these qualities too, it might explain the failure of some replication attempts. In a famous two-experimenter study, Donald West of Cambridge University obtained null results while his colleague, Fisk, was successful (West, 1954). There have been many suggestions that some experimenters are psi-inhibitory while others have the necessary attitudes or beliefs. That is, there could be a psi-mediated experimenter effect in addition to the more usual effect of the experimenter's personality or way of handling the subjects (Irwin, 1989; White, 1977). Critics argue that the differences are because some experimenters are more careful or carry out better experiments than others and that some experimenters cheat.

This parallels another long-standing issue in parapsychology – whether it is better to use special subjects who can produce powerful effects unpredictably and have to be guarded carefully for fraud, or many ordinary subjects who may produce weak effects over many experiments. There have been many famous special subjects, such as Pavel Stepanek, who could guess the colours of concealed cards, Malcolm Bessent, who took part in many kinds of experiments, Ted Serios, who apparently affected unexposed film, and Uri Geller, whose speciality was bending metal. However, most of the standard methods of contemporary experimental research in parapsychology now use unselected subjects. The most important of these are the free-response ESP techniques and PK with random number generators (RNGs).

FREE-RESPONSE ESP RESEARCH

One of the constraints of the early Rhine work was that guessing long series of cards was exceedingly boring. Even when results kept coming, the subjects did not enjoy it and more often results were poor. By contrast, reports of psychic dreams, premonitions, and real-life ESP abounded. The challenge was to capture this in the lab.

One of the best known attempts was the ESP-dream research begun by Montague Ullman in 1960. With the development of electroencephalograph (EEG) recording it became possible to detect when a sleeping person was likely to be dreaming. In experiments at the Maimonides Medical Center in New York the subject slept while an agent looked at a randomly chosen target (Ullman, Krippner, & Vaughan, 1973). Unlike the card-guessing experiments, the targets used could be anything from interesting and colourful pictures to multisensory environments. Sometimes dramatic correspondences were found between the dreams the subject reported and the target. Just as in the early thought transference experiments, this presented a problem of assessment. With such a large amount of material and complex targets, some stunning correspondences are only to be expected, but how many? The solution, and one which has been used in many forms since, was to provide a set of possible targets, only one of which was the actual target. On the basis of the dream, the subject or an independent judge could match up the dream imagery with each of the set and try to identify the true target. In this way the results of a free-response experiment could be subjected to simple statistical tests.

In the case of the dream experiments the results for many subjects were better than would be expected by chance. However, other laboratories did not successfully replicate these findings, possibly because it is very time-consuming and expensive to use a dream laboratory, and the method was dropped.

Instead, other free-response methods were developed. One was "remote viewing". In this case one experimenter goes to a randomly selected remote location and stays there, observing or walking about, for a specified length of time. Meanwhile the subject sits comfortably and relaxes, reporting any impressions or images that arise. Afterwards the subject, or an independent judge, tries to match up the impressions with a set of possible target locations and pick the right one. This method was used by Russell Targ and Harold Puthoff (1977) at the Stanford Research Institute in California and was apparently highly successful. However, two psychologists, David Marks and Richard Kammann, failed to replicate the findings and argued that the previous success had been because the transcripts contained clues as to which previous targets had already been used, increasing the chances of a hit. This lead to a controversy in the prestigious journal *Nature* and attempts by others to confirm or refute the relevance of these clues, a controversy which was never entirely resolved (Marks & Kammann, 1980).

Since then others have claimed success with the remote viewing technique and new methods of analysis have been developed including the use of fuzzy sets. It is often argued that if psi is a real power it ought to have practical applications. Betting seems never to have been one of them, and skeptics have pointed out that casinos reliably continue to make money. However, remote viewing has been used in "psychic archaeology" to find lost sites and, in its most controversial application, to predict price fluctuations of silver futures on the stock market. This attempt, by a group called Delphi Associates, initially produced nine consecutive hits and a hefty profit, but subsequent attempts were not so lucrative.

Since then the most successful of the free-response methods has un-doubtedly been the *Ganzfeld* technique, first used for psi experiments in 1974 by Charles Honorton. He argued that the reason ESP occurs in dreams, meditation, and reverie is because they are all states of reduced sensory input and increased internal attention. He tried to find a way to produce such a "psi-conducive state" without the expense of a dream laboratory. His answer was to tape halved ping-pong balls over the subjects' eyes and play soothing sea-sounds or hissing "white noise" through headphones while they lay on a comfortable couch or reclining chair. This is not total sensory deprivation in complete darkness and silence but does deprive the person of patterned input and encourages internal imagery. This, argued Honorton, would be conducive to ESP.

It appeared to be highly successful. He and his team at the Psychophysical Research Laboratories in Princeton, New Jersey, put many subjects into *Ganzfeld* while an agent looked at a randomly chosen target picture. The subjects were able to pick the correct target picture from a set of others more often than would be predicted by chance. Although several other researchers were unable to replicate the findings, some succeeded, and a replication rate of over 50 per cent was claimed for the technique. Given the problem of replication in parapsychology this appeared to be something of a breakthrough.

In 1982 the "*Ganzfeld* Debate" was launched at a conference marking the centenary of the founding of the Society for Psychical Research. Psychologist Ray Hyman reviewed the entire database and carried out a meta-analysis (in which the results of many similar studies are analysed together). He argued that the replication rate was actually far lower and that there were problems of over-analysis, bias, and many procedural flaws in the experiments. He also found that the most successful studies were those with the most flaws: claims which suggested the entire effect was an artifact (Hyman, 1985). Honorton responded with his own meta-analysis, finding no correlation between the number of flaws and the outcome. In addition, he found that the large effect size was distributed throughout the database and was not dependent on the outstanding results of any one experimenter (Honorton, 1985).

Like many controversies in parapsychology, this one has also never been resolved. However, it led directly to sceptics and parapsychologists coming together to decide what they considered to be serious flaws and what would constitute an acceptable experiment. In the light of these ideas Honorton went on to design a fully automated *Ganzfeld* experiment in which there was little room for any human errors or deliberate fraud. The results of several such experiments were statistically significant and showed consistently better performance using dynamic targets than static ones. When compared to the results of previous meta-analyses, a similar effect size was found and there were better results using senders and receivers who knew each other and who had previous experience of *Ganzfeld* (Honorton et al., 1990). These appear to be consistent and meaningful results that present a real challenge to present-day critics.

Meta-analysis has also been applied to forced-choice studies of precognition. Analysing over 300 studies carried out during a 50-year period, Honorton and Ferrari (1989) found a much smaller effect size than with *Ganzfeld*, but again it was consistent throughout the database and not dependent on study quality. Selective reporting could not explain the effect since they calculated that for each reported study it would need 46 unreported failures to reduce the effect to statistical non-significance. In addition they found that the best results were obtained with short time intervals and with preselected subjects, tested individually and given feedback on their scores.

These findings might suggest that the failure of so many ESP experiments is not because there is no psi but because they have used the easier forced-choice techniques with unselected subjects, tested in groups. The use of meta-analysis constitutes significant progress in that the claims cannot be refuted by finding a single flaw or isolated instance of fraud. They could be undermined only by finding widespread undetected flaws, wholesale cheating, or problems with the meta-analytic techniques themselves.

PK AND RANDOM EVENTS

Psychokinesis (PK) research has come a long way since the studies of table-tipping and levitation. Some have still involved large systems, or macro-PK, such as the attempts to get a purely invented "imaginary ghost" called Philip to levitate tables like an old-fashioned spirit (Owen & Sparrow, 1976); or studies of metal bending with Uri Geller and the many children who emulated him; and studies of the influence on biological systems by William Braud at the Mind Science Foundation in Texas (Braud & Schlitz, 1989). However, by far the majority of research has turned to micro-PK, the supposed effect of the human mind on microscopic, quantum mechanical, or probabilistic systems.

In 1970, Helmut Schmidt, at the Durham Institute for Parapsychology, began work with a new kind of PK machine. The subject's task was to watch a circle of nine lamps and make whichever lamp was lit move clockwise or anti-clockwise. Although the subject did not need to know anything about the mechanism, it actually used a strontium-90 radioactive source emitting particles at random intervals and a Geiger counter to detect them. Since then many other kinds of PK machine have been used and have made it possible to tackle some tricky questions.

For example, what is the difference between PK and precognition? Whenever subjects successfully predict an outcome it is possible to say that instead of using precognition they have actually used PK and brought the event about. This may seem impossible or just unacceptable if the event is a natural disaster or a plane crash, but in experimental situations it seems quite plausible. Schmidt designed a special experiment in which the random number generator was wired up in different ways to test either precognition or PK but the difference could not be detected by the subject (Schmidt & Pantas, 1972). In other experiments the link between the particles emitted and the display that the subject saw was either simple or complex. In either case it seemed to make no difference. Psi seemed to be goal-oriented rather than dependent on the nature of the underlying task.

Another concerned the moment at which the psi is supposed to occur. According to one type of theory, the observational theories, it is the moment of feedback to the subject that is important, not the moment at which the particles are emitted. The display the subject sees and the motivation or concentration at that time are what counts. If this were so it should be possible to delay feedback and still get PK effects. In 1976 Schmidt reported successful results with pre-recorded targets. A radioactive source was used to generate random numbers, and these were converted into clicks on an audio tape or movements of a needle. The subject had to try to influence the clicks to be more in the left or right ear, more strong or weak clicks, or whatever. The strange thing was that the tapes had been made hours, days, or even weeks before. To refute the possibility that subjects might be actually changing the tape by PK, copies of the original output were kept, unseen by anyone, and compared after the experiment was completed. Even more extraordinary was that when some subjects were given the same targets four times over, the effect was stronger, again implying that it was the feedback to the subjects that was important (Schmidt, 1976).

If time-displaced PK seems impossible or nonsensical it is worth bearing in mind that all forms of psi are, from some perspectives, impossible, and this is why the controversies over psi have been so heated and apparently insoluble. The micro-PK experiments have never been so successful with experimenters other than Schmidt, leading some to reject them, but recently Schmidt has designed a PK experiment in which outside observers are needed for crucial phases. This ensures that he alone could not product significant results by cheating. It would need all the people involved to be in collusion. The first experiment of this kind produced a fairly small, but still significant, effect (Schmidt, Morris, & Rudolph, 1986).

Although other PK researchers have not replicated Schmidt's findings, they have developed related machines to act as random event generators (REGs). At the Princeton Engineering Anomalies Research Lab (PEAR) Bob Jahn and his colleagues have collected enormous amounts of data using quantum mechanical REGs. Subjects have some trials in which they have to influence the REG in one direction, some in the opposite direction, and others baseline or resting trials. This allows for comparisons to rule out any bias in the machine itself; all the data ever collected are automatically recorded so that data selection cannot influence the results. The results have produced a tiny, but apparently reliable, deviation from chance expectation.

It is difficult to know how to interpret results such as these. They do not appear to be anything like the classic idea of a mental influence on a physical system, and if they are it must be an extremely weak one. Some parapsychologists interpret it as a mental effect that changes the probabilities of quantum mechanical events. Another approach is that psi is used to bring about desired outcomes, both in ordinary life and experiments, through a "psi-mediated instrumental response" (Stanford, 1990). Ed May at Stanford Research Institute has developed the theory of "intuitive data sorting", which suggests that subjects obtain the desired outcome by selecting the right starting-point for a series of trials rather than influencing each random event in turn. These theories each lead to different testable predictions about the distribution of scores in psi experiments (Walker, 1987).

Critics argue that the effects are very weak, confined to a few investigators, and are probably statistical or experimental artifacts and not paranormal at all. As in the case of the *Ganzfeld*, meta-analysis has been applied. Dean Radin and Roger Nelson (1989) analysed the results of over 800 studies and found chance results in control conditions but deviations from chance in experimental conditions. This effect, though exceedingly small in size, was consistent throughout the database, not related to methodological quality and not dependent on the work of just a few investigators. They conclude that there is an effect of consciousness on physical systems. This connection to consciousness seems unwarranted as yet and it might better be described as an effect of intention.

Alternatively, it could be argued that the relevant flaws have not been found, the chance model with which the effects are compared is inappropriate, or even that an anomaly without a firm theoretical basis is not of interest. Whatever its explanation turns out to be, there does at least seem to be an anomaly in need of explanation, and this is generally the conclusion drawn from other meta-analyses in parapsychology (Utts, 1991).

PSYCHIC EXPERIENCES

The other major areas of parapsychology deal mainly with experiences outside the laboratory. Some odd experiences are not usually considered part of parapsychology, such as sightings of UFOs or strange creatures, earth mysteries, hypnotic regression, fire-walking, astrology, and fortune telling, although some of these have attracted serious study (Frazier, 1991). Those which do form part of parapsychology include spontaneous cases of apparent telepathy, clairvoyance or precognition; psychic dreams and premonitions; poltergeists, apparitions, and hauntings; and out-of-body and near-death experiences.

SPONTANEOUS CASES

Spontaneous cases of telepathy or precognition are notoriously difficult to verify convincingly. The problems of memory distortions and relying on witnesses' reports have been known since the early days and never entirely overcome; perhaps this is why such investigations are rare in modern parapsychology. Attempts have been made to establish premonitions bureaux to which people could send their predictions before they come true, but these have not produced strong evidence of successful prediction. However, many people continue to report apparently psychic experiences. Indeed, personal experience is often given as the main reason for believing in the paranormal, and surveys show that about 50 per cent of the population believe in ESP (Gallup & Newport, 1991).

Possibly this belief reflects the occurrence of genuine psychic events, but other alternatives have been studied. For example Susan Blackmore has suggested that the fact that people underestimate chance probabilities underlies their tendency to interpret ordinary coincidences as psychic events and so bolster their belief. In line with this she found that sheep were more biased

13

in their probability judgements than goats, a finding subsequently confirmed by others (Blackmore & Troscianko, 1985; Brugger, Landis, & Regard, 1990). Other studies have found poorer reasoning skills in believers (Wierzbicki, 1985). Another approach relates psychic and mystical experiences to instability in the temporal lobes. Several studies have found that people with more temporal lobe epileptic signs also report more subjective paranormal experiences (Neppe, 1990; Persinger & Makarec, 1987). Possibly this is due to an increase in a spurious sense of familiarity (as in *déjà vu*) or of emotional salience associated with temporal lobe activity.

Poltergeists have been a traditional area for field research. They are distinguished from apparitions, in which spirits of the dead, or sometimes the living, are apparently seen, and hauntings, in which odd phenomena occur in specific locations.

Parapsychologists have come to regard poltergeists as caused not by the spirits of the dead but by the living, and hence they are sometimes referred to as recurrent spontaneous psychokinesis (RSPK). A review of 500 cases, going back to the sixteenth century, shows features they have in common, in particular the unexplained movements of objects (Gauld & Cornell, 1979). Objects are sometimes seen actually flying around, though the beginning of the movement is rarely observed. Often there are unexplained noises, doors opening and closing, and occasionally, as in the Enfield case in north London, levitation of people. Often, but not invariably, the focus of activity is a teenager or sometimes younger children. In the famous Rosenheim case in Germany, an 18-year-old secretary in a lawyer's office was apparently the centre of extraordinary movements of objects, explosions in the light fittings and fuses, and a total disruption of the telephone system. Electricians and telephone engineers were unable to discover the cause of the disturbance. In another well-known case a Miami novelty warehouse was plagued by movements and breakages centring on a 19-year-old Cuban refugee. Although he was said to be unhappy and had been arrested for shop-lifting, and was naturally under suspicion, he was never observed throwing the souvenirs himself (Gauld & Cornell, 1979).

Poltergeist focuses are often said to be unstable, suffering psychological conflict, or living in difficult family situations. A connection to epilepsy has also been suggested, but poltergeists are hard to study and the data far from conclusive. Of course in many putative poltergeist cases the children or adult focus are suspected of fraud, and in some, such as one instance in Cleveland, Ohio, they are caught red-handed. In this case it was a journalist's films which revealed the child throwing a telephone across the room when no one was looking (Randi, 1985). There has been a long history of fraudulent children in psychical research (Nicol, 1985). It is certain that many otherwise astute scientists have been duped by such tricks and that it is not always possible to detect them. Whether all poltergeists are due to trickery is very much a matter of dispute.

OUT-OF-BODY EXPERIENCES

Another phenomenon traditionally studied by parapsychologists but now increasingly becoming part of psychology, is the out-of-body experience (OBE). About 10 per cent of the population claims to have had this experience at least once in their life. Typically they seem to be viewing the world from a location outside their body. It feels as though they, their "spirit", "soul", or "centre of consciousness", has temporarily left the body and is able to travel around without it. OBEs often occur in times of stress, sensory deprivation, deep relaxation, or when close to death. They are often very brief, although some people can learn to induce them at will and take control. The world seen during an OBE is extremely vivid and realistic, and OBEs sometimes claim to see things at a distance that they could not possibly have known about (Blackmore, 1982).

Traditionally, these experiences have been described as "astral projection" in which the astral body leaves the physical. Parapsychologists have tried with little success to find evidence that this other body is detectable or can actually see things. Alternative psychological theories have recently been developed to try to account for the experience in terms of changes in the body image or reconstructions from memory and imagination (Blackmore, 1993; Irwin, 1985).

SURVIVAL OF DEATH

Research into apparitions at the moment of death, mediumistic communication, and other apparent forms of evidence for survival still continue, but not to the extent they did in the early days of psychical research. One problem that has never been resolved is known as the super-ESP hypothesis. If the possibility of ESP and PK is admitted then any evidence that purports to come from a discarnate being could alternatively be said to come from the psi powers of the living. This may have to entail ridiculously complex or powerful forms of ESP, unlike anything seen in the lab (hence the name super-ESP), nevertheless it is always an alternative which makes finding evidence for survival next to impossible.

Attempts have been made to get round this. In the famous "cross-correspondences", during the first three decades of the twentieth century, several mediums independently produced allusions to the same things at the same time, purportedly coming from Frederick Myers (see above) among others, and including obscure but meaningful literary references (Gauld, 1982). Communications like this do not seem to happen today. However, some people are still trying to prove survival. One method is to leave behind a combination lock which can be opened only when the correct number is communicated through a medium. Another is to create a coded message for which the cipher is known to only one person. So far these techniques have not produced any successes.

Another kind of evidence, sometimes said to indicate survival, comes from near-death experiences (NDEs). These are experiences reported by people who have been close to death but have survived. NDErs typically feel peaceful and even joyful. They often seem to float or rush quickly down a dark tunnel with a bright light at the end. The light is warm and even friendly. It may seem like a person greeting them or asking questions to help them evaluate their life and its meaning. Often the experience includes an OBE in which the person seems to observe attempts at resuscitation, or whatever else is going on, from a distance. In the longest or deepest NDEs people may enter other worlds of love and beauty, meet dead friends or relatives, and have experiences which seem to be of mystical understanding and acceptance. Often they report being changed for the better, becoming more caring and less materialistic afterwards.

NDEs were first described in detail by the American physician Raymond Moody (1975), although many isolated cases had been reported before that. Subsequently, more detailed research has confirmed that the experiences take a consistent form and are independent of the cause of the close brush with death or the drugs taken at the time. Indeed it is possible to have all the features of the NDE without being physically close to death, for example in climbers who fall but land safely, or people who think they are about to die but in fact are not. Some researchers argue that the NDE is a glimpse of the afterlife or an alternative reality (Ring, 1980). If something leaves the body in out-of-body experiences, it is argued, that "something" might survive after the physical body is truly dead.

Others argue that the experience is a product of the dying brain. For example drugs such as LSD or even nitrous oxide can induce comparable experiences; the tunnel can be explained by the random firing that occurs in the visual cortex as the brain dies, the blissful feelings may be related to the release of endorphin (a natural opiate in the brain) under stress, and the OBE can be understood in psychological terms (Blackmore, 1993). Many of the phenomena are similar to those induced by temporal lobe stimulation, and it is known that the endorphins released during fear and stress can lead to temporal lobe seizures. Evidence against such explanations is the claim that people during NDEs are able to see things they could not possibly have heard or known about. However, there are very few cases of this kind and even these are very hard to substantiate (Blackmore, 1993). As has occurred in many other areas, what looked like evidence for life after death can be interpreted in alternative ways, in this case ways that also increase our understanding of brain function. Evidence for survival, though often claimed, is elusive.

CRITICISM AND SCEPTICISM

Right from the start of parapsychology there have been constructive critics who have helped it develop the necessary methodological rigour, and extreme critics who have made unwarranted accusations and preferred any alternative to the possibility of the paranormal. Many of the first critics in the 1940s were silenced by the progressing research, but in 1955 a paper in the prestigious journal *Science* argued that "just one good experiment" was still needed (Price, 1955). In the mid-1960s the Swansea psychologist Mark Hansel (1966) argued that most of the impressive results so far could have been obtained by fraud, and he suggested how subjects or experimenters could have looked through windows, used trap doors, or in other ways circumvented the experimental controls. Many parapsychologists felt that these suggestions were far-fetched, but the subsequent exposure of Soal's trickery showed how carefully experiments need to be evaluated.

During the 1970s the issues were argued in the pages of a psychology journal (Moss & Butler, 1978; Rao, 1979), and in the 1980s in the peer review journal, *Behavioral and Brain Sciences* (Alcock, 1987). As well as the British and American Societies for Psychical Research, and the professional Parapsychological Association, there is also now a powerful sceptical organization called the Committee for the Scientific Investigation of Claims of the Paranormal (CSICOP) and many local sceptical groups. Although many of the best researchers are not interested in taking sides and actively encourage cooperation between researchers and critics, the arguments do not appear to be dying down.

After over a century of research into the paranormal, there are very few definite conclusions to be drawn. The methods used have become increasingly sophisticated, as have the types of criticism required. Meta-analyses of large areas of research claim to have found consistent, if weak, effects. We have yet to see whether these herald a new era of progress for this controversial science.

FURTHER READING

Alcock, J. E. (1981). *Parapsychology: Science or magic?* Oxford: Pergamon.
Broughton, R. S. (1991). *Parapsychology: The controversial science.* New York: Ballantine.
Edge, H. L., Morris, R. L., Palmer, J., & Rush, J. H. (1986). *Foundations of parapsychology: Exploring the boundaries of human capability.* London: Routledge & Kegan Paul.
Irwin, H. J. (1989). *An introduction to parapsychology.* Jefferson, NC: McFarland.
Kurtz, P. (1985). *A skeptic's handbook of parapsychology.* Buffalo, NY: Prometheus.

REFERENCES

Alcock, J. E. (1981). *Parapsychology: Science or magic?* Oxford: Pergamon.

Alcock, J. E. (1987). Parapsychology: Science of the anomalous or search for the soul? *Behavioral and Brain Sciences, 10,* 553–643 (including commentary by other authors).

Blackmore, S. J. (1982). *Beyond the body: An investigation of out-of-the-body experiences.* London: Heinemann.

Blackmore, S. J. (1993). *Dying to live: Science and the near-death experience.* London: Grafton.

Blackmore, S. J., & Troscianko, T. S. (1985). Belief in the paranormal: Probability judgements, illusory control, and the "chance baseline shift". *British Journal of Psychology, 76,* 459–468.

Boring, E. G. (1966). Introduction. In C. E. M. Hansel, *ESP: A scientific evaluation* (pp. xiii–xxi). New York: Scribners.

Brandon, R. (1983). *The spiritualists.* London: Weidenfeld & Nicolson.

Braud, W., & Schlitz, M. (1989). A methodology for the objective study of transpersonal imagery. *Journal of Scientific Exploration, 3,* 43–63.

Broughton, R. S. (1991). *Parapsychology: The controversial science.* New York: Ballantine.

Brugger, P., Landis, T., & Regard, M. (1990). A "sheep-goat effect" in repetition avoidance: Extra-sensory perception as an effect of subjective probability? *British Journal of Psychology, 81,* 455–468.

Coover, J. E. (1917). *Experiments in psychical research at Leland Stanford Junior University,* Psychical Research Monograph, Stanford, CA: Leland Stanford University Publications.

Faraday, M. (1853). Experimental investigation of table-moving. *The Athenaeum,* July, 801–803.

Frazier, K. (Ed.) (1991). *The hundredth monkey and other paradigms of the paranormal.* Buffalo, NY: Prometheus.

Gallup, G. H., & Newport, F. (1991). Belief in paranormal phenomena among adult Americans. *Skeptical Inquirer, 15,* 137–146.

Gauld, A. (1968). *The founders of psychical research.* London: Routledge & Kegan Paul.

Gauld, A. (1982). *Mediumship and survival: A century of investigations.* London: Heinemann.

Gauld, A., & Cornell, A. D. (1979). *Poltergeists.* London: Routledge & Kegan Paul.

Grattan-Guinness, I. (1982). *Psychical research: A guide to its history, principles and practices.* Wellingborough, Northants: Aquarian.

Gurney, E., Myers, F. W. H., & Podmore, F. (1886). *Phantasms of the living.* London: Trubner.

Hansel, C. E. M. (1966). *ESP: A scientific evaluation.* New York: Scribners.

Honorton, H. (1985). A meta-analysis of psi ganzfeld research: A response to Hyman. *Journal of Parapsychology, 49,* 51–91.

Honorton, C., & Ferrari, D. C. (1989). "Future telling": A meta-analysis of forced-choice precognition experiments, 1935–1987. *Journal of Parapsychology, 53,* 281–308.

Honorton, H., Berger, R. E., Varvoglis, M. P., Quant, M., Derr, P. Schechter, E. I., & Ferrari, D. C. (1990). Psi communication in the ganzfeld: Experiments with an automated testing system and a comparison with a meta-analysis of earlier studies. *Journal of Parapsychology, 54,* 99–139.

Hyman, R. (1985). The Ganzfeld psi experiment: A critical appraisal. *Journal of Parapsychology, 49*, 3–49.

Irwin, H. J. (1985). *Flight of mind: A psychological study of the out-of-body experience*. Metuchen, NJ: Scarecrow.

Irwin, H. J. (1989). *An introduction to parapsychology*. Jefferson, NC: McFarland.

Marks, D., & Kammann, R. (1980). *The psychology of the psychic*. Buffalo, NY: Prometheus.

Markwick, B. (1978). The Soal-Goldney experiments with Basil Shackleton: New evidence of data manipulation. *Proceedings of the Society for Psychical Research, 56*, 250–281.

Mauskopf, S. H., & McVaugh, M. R. (1980). *The elusive science: Origins of experimental psychical research*. Baltimore, MD: Johns Hopkins University Press.

Moody, R. (1975). *Life after life*. Covinda, GA: Mockingbird.

Moss, S., & Butler, D. C. (1978). The scientific credibility of ESP. *Perceptual and Motor Skills, 46*, 1063–1079.

Neppe, V. M. (1990). Anomalistic experience and the cerebral cortex. In S. Krippner (Ed.) *Advances in parapsychological research* (vol. 6, pp. 168–183). Jefferson, NC: McFarland.

Nicol, J. F. (1985). Fraudulent children in psychical research. In P. Kurtz (Ed.) *A skeptic's handbook of parapsychology* (pp. 275–286). Buffalo, NY: Prometheus.

Owen, I. M., & Sparrow, M. (1976). *Conjuring up Philip: An adventure in psychokinesis*. Toronto: Fitzhenry & Whiteside.

Palmer, J. (1971). Scoring in ESP tests as a function of belief in ESP. Part 1: The sheep–goat effect. *Journal of the American Society for Psychical Research, 65*, 373–408.

Persinger, M. A., & Makarec, K. (1987). Temporal lobe epileptic signs and correlative behaviours displayed by normal populations. *Journal of General Psychology, 114*, 179–195.

Podmore, F. (1902). *Modern spiritualism: A history and a criticism*. London: Methuen.

Price, G. R. (1955). Science and the supernatural. *Science, 122*, 359–367.

Radin, D. I., & Nelson, R. D. (1989). Evidence for consciousness-related anomalies in random physical systems. *Foundations of Physics, 19*, 1499–1514.

Randi, J. (1975). *The truth about Uri Geller*. Buffalo, NY: Prometheus.

Randi, J. (1985). The Columbus poltergeist case: Part 1. *Skeptical Inquirer, 9*, 221–235.

Rao, K. R. (1979). On "The scientific credibility of ESP". *Perceptual and Motor Skills, 49*, 415–429.

Rhine, J. B. (1934). *Extrasensory perception*. Boston, MA: Bruce Humphries.

Rhine, J. B. (1947). *The reach of the mind*. New York: Sloane.

Rhine, J. B. (1969). Position effects in psi test results. *Journal of Parapsychology, 33*, 136–157.

Rhine, L. E. (1981). *The invisible picture: A study of psychic experiences*. Jefferson, NC: McFarland.

Ring, K. (1980). *Life at death*. New York: Coward, McCann & Geoghegan.

Schmeidler, G. R., & McConnell, R. A. (1958). *ESP and personality patterns*. New Haven, CT: Yale University Press.

Schmidt, H. (1976). PK effect on pre-recorded targets. *Journal of the American Society for Psychical Research, 70*, 267–292.

Schmidt, H., & Pantas, L. (1972). PK tests with internally different machines. *Journal of Parapsychology, 36*, 222–232.

Schmidt, H., Morris, R., & Rudolph, L. (1986). Channeling evidence for a PK effect to independent observers. *Journal of Parapsychology*, *50*, 1–15.

Soal, S. G., & Bateman, F. (1954). *Modern experiments in telepathy*. London: Faber & Faber.

Stanford, R. (1990). An experimentally testable model for spontaneous psi events: A review of related evidence and concepts from parapsychology and other sciences. In S. Krippner (Ed.) *Advances in parapsychological research* (vol. 6, pp. 54–167). Jefferson, NC: McFarland.

Targ, R., & Puthoff, H. (1977). *Mind-reach*. New York: Delacorte.

Thalbourne, M. A. (1982). *A glossary of terms used in parapsychology*. London: Heinemann.

Ullman, M., Krippner, S., & Vaughan, A. (1973). *Dream telepathy*. London: Turnstone.

Utts, J. (1991). Replication and meta-analysis in parapsychology. *Statistical Science*, *6*, 363–403 (with comments by other authors).

Walker, E. H. (1987). A comparison of the intuitive data sorting and quantum mechanical observer theories. *Journal of Parapsychology*, *51*, 217–227.

West, D. (1954). *Psychical research today*. London: Duckworth.

White, R. A. (1977). The influence of the experimenter motivation, attitudes and methods of handling subjects in psi test results. In B. Wolman (Ed.) *Handbook of parapsychology* (pp. 273–303). Jefferson, NC: McFarland.

Wierzbicki, M. (1985). Reasoning errors and belief in the paranormal. *Journal of Social Psychology*, *125*, 489–494.

11.2

HYPNOSIS

Graham F. Wagstaff

University of Liverpool, England

Although some writers claim that hypnotic techniques can be traced back to ancient times, it is more often assumed that the origins of modern hypnosis are to be found in the practitioners of "magnetic medicine", in particular Franz Anton Mesmer (1734–1815). Mesmer proposed that the human body was filled with a magnetic fluid, that disease resulted from a disequilibrium in this fluid, and that by using techniques with his patients, such as making passes over them, touching them, and staring into their eyes, he could correct this disequilibrium and effect cures. However, in 1784 two commissions were appointed to investigate Mesmer's activities, they concluded that the alleged magnetic phenomena were simply the result of imagination (Wagstaff, 1981).

The coining of the term "hypnosis" itself (derived from the Greek *hypnos* or sleep) is usually attributed to the Manchester surgeon James Braid (1795–1860), although the term "hypnotism" is to be found in French dictionaries published several decades before Braid's principal work (Gravitz & Gerton, 1984). Braid, like some previous observers of mesmerism, had concluded that mesmerized subjects had fallen into a sleep-like state. This idea was then developed most notably by the French neurologist Jean Charcot (1825–1893), who asserted that the hypnotic state was an hysterical condition that involved three stages, lethargy, catalepsy, and somnambulism. A famous and very vigorous disagreement then arose between Charcot and his followers at the Salpêtrière hospital, and Hippolyte Bernheim (1840–1919) and his followers at the University of Nancy. Bernheim proposed that hypnosis is a non-pathological state and that hypnotic phenomena are primarily the result of suggestion; indeed, he argued that the hypnotic induction ritual does not necessarily enhance the effectiveness of suggestion.

The role of imagination and suggestion in hypnosis has continued to be a source of considerable controversy, to the extent that some contemporary theorists contend that to explain hypnotic phenomena we do not need to postulate an hypnotic state at all. As a result a continuing debate exists between those theorists, often loosely referred to as "state" theorists, who adhere to the notion of hypnosis as an altered state of consciousness, and "non-state" theorists, who reject this notion (Fellows, 1990).

HYPNOSIS AS AN ALTERED STATE

According to the classic state view, hypnosis is seen as an altered state of consciousness with various depths, such that the deeper one enters the hypnotic state the more likely one is to manifest hypnotic phenomena (Bowers, 1983). This state is alleged by some to occur spontaneously, but it is normally brought about through induction procedures, such as eye fixation and vocal suggestions for sleep and relaxation. In academic research, susceptibility to hypnosis is usually measured by means of standardized scales; commonly used are the Stanford Hypnotic Susceptibility Scale (forms A, B, and C), and the Harvard Group Scale of Hypnotic Susceptibility. These scales usually start off with an induction ritual followed by various suggestions, such as hand lowering ("Your hand is heavy and falling"), amnesia ("You will find it difficult to remember"), and sometimes an hallucination ("There is a fly buzzing round your head").

Most modern state theorists contend that hypnosis is an altered state of consciousness that enables subjects to release the "dissociative" capacities that lie within them (see e.g., J. Barber, 1991). Of these approaches, undoubtedly the most influential is Hilgard's "neo-dissociation theory" (Hilgard, 1986, 1991). Basing his ideas on those of the early dissociationists such as Prince and Janet, Hilgard argues that there exist multiple systems of control that are not all conscious at the same time. Normally these cognitive control systems are under the influence of a central control structure, or "executive ego", that controls and monitors the other systems; but when a subject enters hypnosis, the hypnotist takes away much of the normal control and monitoring such that, in response to suggestion, motor movements are experienced as involuntary, memory and perception are distorted, and hallucinations are perceived as real. To demonstrate this principle, Hilgard frequently refers to the "hidden-observer" phenomenon, whereby a subject is "hypnotized" and given the following instruction:

> When I place my hand on your shoulder, I shall be able to talk to a hidden part of you that knows things are going on in your body, things that are unknown to the part of you to which I am now talking. The part to which I am now talking will not know what you are telling me or even that you are talking. . . . You will remember that there is a part of you that knows many things that are going on that may be hidden from either your normal consciousness or the hypnotized part of you. (Knox, Morgan, & Hilgard, 1974, p. 842)

Hilgard and his associates claim that, using this technique on "hypnotized" subjects, they are able to access, or talk to, other control systems of which the subject might otherwise be unaware.

The concept at dissociation is particularly useful for state theorists as it provides a possible explanation for two of the fundamental assumptions of the traditional view of hypnosis: first, when "under hypnosis", subjects typically experience suggested effects as involuntary "happenings", not as deliberate, voluntary activities, and second, hypnotic performance can transcend normal waking performance, or at least hypnotic procedures enable subjects to experience effects in a unique or unusual way; thus, for example, most state theorists accept that hypnotized subjects possess a special capacity to control pain and can experience amnesia and hallucinations in a unique way (Bowers, 1983; Bowers & Davidson, 1991; Hilgard & Hilgard, 1983).

The state view has tended to dominate the popular conception of hypnosis, and perhaps one of the major reasons for this is the dramatic nature of many hypnotic phenomena; for example, "hypnotized" subjects can allegedly tolerate surgery without pain, regress back to childhood with great accuracy, be made deaf, blind, and amnesic, hallucinate objects and people "as real as real", and perform complex tasks without awareness of doing so. Such phenomena might suggest that some rather exotic process is at work in hypnosis. However, the idea of hypnosis as an altered state has been subject to a concerted attack from those who deny that any special process is involved.

THE NON-STATE APPROACH

Scepticism concerning the notion of hypnosis as an altered state has mounted since the 1960s (see, e.g., T. X. Barber, 1969; Sarbin & Coe, 1972; Spanos, 1991; Wagstaff, 1981). Although they differ in their emphases, non-state theorists argue that hypnotic phenomena are readily explicable in terms of more mundane psychological concepts, mainly from the areas of social and cognitive psychology, such as attitudes, expectancies, beliefs, compliance, imagination, attention, concentration, distraction, and relaxation.

To many non-state theorists the hypnotic situation is best seen as a social interaction in which both hypnotist and subject enact roles; the role of the hypnotic subjects being to present themselves as "hypnotized" according to previous expectations and cues available in the immediate situation. This does not mean that hypnotic behaviours are necessarily faked or sham (though some may be); the subject may become very involved in the role and may use a variety of strategies to successfully bring about the desired effects. For example, in response to an arm-lowering suggestion, subjects may try to imagine weights on the arm, or if amnesia is suggested, they may try to forget by employing a distraction strategy. In fact, Wagstaff (1991) has proposed that hypnotic responding may involve three stages. First, the subject figures out what is expected on the basis of previous experience and the hypnotist's instructions. Second, the subject employs imaginative or other strategies to try to bring about the suggested effects, and third, if the strategies fail, or are judged to be inappropriate, the subject either gives up, or reverts to behavioural compliance or faking. Non-state theorists thus question the assumption that hypnotic behaviour is automatic; for example, according to Wagstaff (1981) much alleged involuntary behaviour may simply be a pretence, and Spanos (1986a, 1991) argues that, because non-volition is implied in hypnotic suggestions, subjects may try to actively redefine what is in fact voluntary behaviour as involuntary. Non-state theorists also reject the notion that hypnotic behaviour can transcend "waking" behaviour.

The problem of compliance, or faking, in hypnosis is one recognized by both state and non-state theorists, largely as a result of the pioneering work of Orne (1959, 1966), who emphasized the extent to which subjects in any experimental context may modify their behaviour in an attempt to please the experimenter, save themselves from embarrassment, or bolster their self-image. However, to some non-state theorists compliance is not just an annoyance in hypnosis research, it may be seen as an integral component of much hypnotic responding (Spanos, 1991; Wagstaff, 1991). Such ideas raise some difficult semantic issues; for instance, are non-state theorists saying that "hypnosis" actually does not exist? There is no simple answer to this question; however, most non-state theorists continue to use the words "hypnosis" or "hypnotic" operationally, to refer to any context defined by those participating in it as "hypnosis". Thus a "hypnotic" group would be one that has been given a hypnotic induction procedure, and "hypnotized" or "hypnotically susceptible" subjects are those who tend to respond positively to suggestions in what is defined as a hypnotic context. From this non-state perspective, therefore, "hypnosis" does exist, but as a label for a context rather than as an altered state of consciousness (see, e.g., Spanos, 1989; Wagstaff, 1991).

The methodological problems involved in deciding between the state and non-state viewpoints are immense and have given rise to some highly innovative experimental research designs. The basic approach has been to compare subjects who have been given an hypnotic induction procedure with various control groups designed to test alternative non-state explanations. At the forefront has been Orne's (1979) "real-simulator" design, in which "hypnotized" subjects are compared with subjects instructed to fake excellent hypnotic subjects, but without any explicit instructions as to how this is to be accomplished. Another popular control group has been T. X. Barber's (1969) "task-motivated" group; in this subjects are told to try hard to imagine and experience hypnotic suggestions, but without a formal induction procedure. The logic behind these approaches is that if no differences emerge between the hypnotic and control groups, then it is not necessary to propose a special hypnotic process, or state, to explain the responses of the hypnotic subjects; on the other hand, if differences do occur, it may be reasonable to assume that hypnotic induction may add a special element.

THE PHYSIOLOGY OF HYPNOSIS

If hypnosis is a special state of consciousness, perhaps related to sleep, it would be useful to know whether "hypnotized" subjects would manifest any physiological changes not shown by non-hypnotic control subjects. A wide variety of measures have been investigated, including EEG, blood pressure and chemistry, respiration rate, and skin temperature and resistance. Although the search continues (see, e.g., Gruzelier, 1988), most researchers of both state and non-state persuasion now seem to agree that the quest to find a unique correlate of the hypnotic state has not been very successful. Physiological changes do often occur following hypnotic induction or hypnotic suggestions, but they seem to be explicable in other ways; for example, they may be due simply to normal changes in attention (Jones & Flynn, 1989), or the achievement of a relaxed state (Edmonston, 1991). This latter finding invites an obvious question; is hypnosis simply a state of relaxation? At first it would seem that hypnosis and relaxation are not equivalent because subjects can appear "hypnotized" when involved in strenuous activities, such as pedalling an exercise bike (Malott, 1984). Nevertheless, Edmonston (1991) has argued that one can still be relaxed (cognitively) even when engaged in physical activity. However, perhaps the main problem with the notion that hypnosis is just relaxation is that it does not adequately explain how various hypnotic phenomena, such as hallucinations and amnesia, arise (Fellows, 1990).

TRANSCENDENT PROPERTIES OF HYPNOSIS

Part of the popular conception of hypnosis is that it enables individuals to transcend their normal capacities. Some early claims were very dramatic; for example, it was once believed that hypnotic subjects could see with the backs of their heads, see through the skin to the internal organs, and communicate with the dead (Spanos, 1982). It has also been claimed that hypnosis can enable people to relive past lives (Wagstaff, 1981). Although such dramatic claims tend not to be taken seriously by academic researchers, less exaggerated claims continue to be made. For instance, claims have been made that hypnosis may be particularly valuable in the forensic context for helping victims and eyewitnesses to remember details of crimes; however, most evidence suggests that hypnosis does not facilitate memory more than other procedures that encourage the vivid recollection of details; in fact, sometimes hypnosis may simply encourage witnesses to confabulate, or make up details (Wagstaff, 1989).

Work in this area has emphasized many of the pitfalls in research into hypnosis. Often observers of demonstrations of hypnosis are unaware of the capacities of the average person, which go untested; for example, most people are quite able to perform the apparent transcendent feats in stage demonstrations of hypnosis without any attempt to employ an hypnotic procedure (T. X. Barber, Spanos, & Chaves, 1974); these include not showing outward expressions of pain in response to a noxious stimulus, and the ability of a subject to support the weight of one or even two individuals while suspended between two chairs – one under the shoulders, the other under the calves. In experimental and clinical research an important difficulty arises when attempts are made to compare the performance of the *same* subjects in both hypnotic and non-hypnotic conditions; in these circumstances subjects may tend to underperform or "hold back" in the non-hypnotic condition so that when they are "hypnotized" their performance will appear to have improved (Wagstaff, 1981). Using more appropriate experimental designs, such as using independent groups of simulators or task-motivated subjects, some of the earlier claims for hypnosis seem to be unsubstantiated; for example, there is no conclusive evidence that hypnotic subjects are superior to suitably motivated non-hypnotic subjects on a range of tasks including appearing deaf, blind, and colour blind, acting like a child and recalling events from childhood, producing perceptual effects while "hallucinating", lifting weights and other athletic tasks, showing improvements in eyesight, and learning and remembering (T. X. Barber, 1969; Jacobs & Gotthelf, 1986; Jones & Flynn, 1989; Wagstaff, 1981). Even when tasks involve dangerous or antisocial activities, subjects simulating hypnosis are just as likely, and occasionally more likely, to perform them than hypnotic or "real" subjects; such tasks have included picking up a poisonous snake, putting one's hand into a glass of concentrated acid and throwing the acid at the experimenter, peddling heroin, mutilating the Bible, and making slanderous statements (Wagstaff, 1981, 1989).

As attempts to demonstrate that hypnosis enables individuals to transcend their normal capacities have generally failed or been inconclusive, researchers have turned their attention to more subtle differences between hypnotic and non-hypnotic behaviour and experience. For example, one possible way of determining whether hypnotic behaviours are influenced by experimental demands would be to see if they still occur when the hypnotist is not present. In one investigation, Orne, Sheehan, and Evans (1968) found that some hypnotic subjects continued to respond to a posthypnotic suggestion (to touch their foreheads on hearing the word "experiment"), even when the hypnotist was not present, whereas simulators stopped responding in the absence of the hypnotist. However, other investigators have found that when subjects are tested totally outside the experimental setting, by someone who ostensibly has nothing whatsoever to do with the experiment, the post-hypnotic responses disappear entirely (Spanos, Menary, Brett, Cross, & Ahmed, 1987). The latter finding appears to fit well with the non-state view, but other phenomena seem less easily dismissed.

TRANCE LOGIC

One of the most controversial issues is that of "trance logic". This term was devised by Orne (1959, 1979) to refer to the observation that "hypnotized" individuals, unlike simulators, appear to have little need for logical consistency and can tolerate illogical responses. Four phenomena, in particular, have been identified as key examples of trance logic. First, when hypnotic subjects ("reals") view a person, and at the same time receive a suggestion to hallucinate the person standing in a different place, they tend to report seeing *both* the actual person and the hallucinated image; however, hardly any simulators do this. Orne (1959) termed this the "double hallucination" response. Second, when hypnotic subjects are shown an empty chair and it is suggested to them that a person is sitting on it, they will tend to report that the image is transparent; that is, they can see the chair through the person. Simulators, however, tend to report an opaque or solid image; they say they cannot see the back of the chair. Third, when given a suggestion to regress back to childhood, some hypnotic subjects will report, alternately or simul-taneously, that they felt both like an adult *and* a child. Fourth, unlike a child, they will correctly write a complex sentence; simulators, on the other hand, will tend to report feeling like a child all the time, and will write the sentence incorrectly, as would a child. These phenomena have been termed "duality" and "incongruous writing" respectively (Nogrady, McConkey, Laurence, & Perry, 1983). In terms of neo-dissociation theory, all of these examples of trance logic could reflect the possibility that, during hypnosis, different "parts" of consciousness are being accessed alternately or simultaneously. It should be noted, however, that not all hypnotically susceptible "reals" display trance logic.

Further research into these phenomena has produced mixed results. According to de Groot and Gwynn (1989), at least nine studies have failed to demonstrate a difference between "reals" and simulators on the double hallucination response; nevertheless, a number of researchers have found that "reals" are indeed more likely to proffer a transparent hallucination response, and display duality and incongruous writing, than simulators. However, non-state theorists have questioned whether these differences between "reals" and simulators are evidence for hypnosis as a special state.

27

One of the difficulties with the traditional real-simulator design is that the two groups operate under different instructions; the simulators are told specifically to behave like *excellent* subjects, whereas the "reals" are not; the latter can behave as "hypnotized" as they wish, and report as honestly as they wish. It could be the case, therefore, that because they are trying to behave like excellent subjects, simulators are more likely to act in an extreme way (Wagstaff, 1981); hence, just like some of the highly susceptible "reals" who do *not* display trance logic, simulators, when asked to hallucinate, will tend to report complete solid hallucinations, and when given suggestions to regress, will report feeling like a child all of the time, and will write like a child. On the other hand, perhaps the "trance-logical reals" use a different strategy; they may simply be exercising their imagination, or offering a less complete or less extreme response. To test this hypothesis, some researchers have used control groups who have been instructed to imagine the various effects, or have been given the same suggestions without hypnotic induction; using these controls no differences have been found between the hypnotic and non-hypnotic groups on the various measures of trance logic (de Groot & Gwynn, 1989; Spanos, 1986a). It has been proposed by state theorists that the non-hypnotic controls in these studies might have inadvertently "slipped into an hypnotic state", but apart from the general difficulty of arguing that, in their everyday lives, people must slip in and out of an hypnotic state whenever they use their imagination, typically imagination controls do not report experiences of being "hypnotized" (Obstoj & Sheehan, 1977).

In opposition to the non-state view on this topic, however, is the finding that hypnotic subjects who display trance logic are also more likely to show the "hidden-observer" effect (Nogrady et al., 1983). If trance logic is simply an incomplete response, or reflects the use of everyday imagination, it seems difficult to see why it should relate to hidden-observer responding; this finding would seem to fit better with a neo-dissociation explanation, in that both trance logic and the production of a "hidden observer" could be construed as examples of the capacity for dissociation under hypnosis. Nevertheless, Spanos, de Groot, Tiller, Weekes, and Bertrand (1985) have failed to replicate this finding, so the issue remains unresolved.

The idea that when hypnotic subjects report transparent hallucinations they may simply be saying they "imagined" what was suggested to them raises the general question of the validity of hypnotic hallucinations. State theorists seem in little doubt that hypnotic subjects can experience hallucinations "as real as real" (Bowers, 1983). Non-state theorists are more sceptical; for example, Spanos (1982) reports that, if given the option, hypnotic subjects will prefer to say their hallucinations were "imagined" rather than seen, and though some subjects continue to maintain they have "seen" suggested hallucinations, so do an equivalent proportion of task-motivated subjects. However, Bowers (1983) argues that, when asked to be honest, task-motivated subjects report less vivid hallucinations than hypnotic subjects.

One of the most extraordinary hypnotic phenomena is the *negative* hallucination, whereby hypnotic subjects maintain that they *cannot* see something placed plainly before their open eyes. According to some state theorists, the visual stimulus is "seen" by one "part" of the mind, but it is somehow blocked from awareness (Zamansky & Bartis, 1985). To some non-state theorists, however, the explanation for this phenomenon is rather more simple: the subjects are lying (Wagstaff, 1991).

HYPNOTIC AMNESIA

Another hotly debated phenomenon is hypnotic amnesia. Typically, if hypnotic subjects are given some suggestions to perform, or a word list to learn, and are told they will forget what they have done or learned, they will show either total or partial forgetting, until a release signal, such as "Now you can remember", is given. It is commonly accepted that hypnotic amnesia is not equivalent to normal forgetting, because some or all of the "forgotten" material can be recovered immediately following the release signal. According to neo-dissociation theory, this happens because temporarily, during hypnosis, the memories are dissociated from conscious control and cannot be accessed voluntarily. Thus, no matter how hard they try, hypnotic subjects cannot remember the material until the release signal is given and normal control is restored (Bowers, 1983; Hilgard, 1986).

Non-state theorists tend to explain hypnotic amnesia differently; they argue that hypnotic subjects interpret the amnesia suggestion as an instruction to avoid remembering. Hence, when they have apparently forgotten, hypnotic subjects are not engaging in fruitless attempts to remember, rather they are deliberately trying *not* to remember. To do this subjects may adopt a number of different strategies; for example, they may simply pretend that they cannot remember, or they may try to avoid remembering by distracting themselves, or making no effort to think about the material (Spanos, 1986a; Wagstaff, 1981).

If the non-state theorists are correct, then presumably it should be possible to "breach" hypnotic amnesia by instructing subjects to tell the truth, or to actively attend to the material. However, Kihlstrom, Evans, Orne, and Orne (1980) found that some hypnotic subjects continued to display amnesia despite such instructions. In response, non-state theorists have argued that some subjects may have such an investment in displaying amnesia that they would "lose face" if they started to remember as a result of such instructions; consequently, to breach amnesia, subjects need either a more powerful stimulus to remember, or to be able to remember without discrediting themselves. In support of this view it has been shown that, in the vast majority of subjects, amnesia can be breached when subjects are asked to be honest, rigged up to a lie detector, and shown a videotape of their performance (Coe, 1989). Wagstaff (1977) demonstrated that amnesia can be eliminated completely if subjects are given an opportunity to say they were "role-playing", rather than in a hypnotic "trance". The fact remains, however, that hypnotic amnesia is difficult to breach entirely, and state theorists can argue that these breaching techniques effectively destroy the influence of the hypnotic state.

A number of other amnesia effects have been investigated. For example, when hypnotic subjects are presented with items in sequence or categories, and are asked to forget them, they sometimes recall them in a disorganized fashion (out of sequence or not in categories); this is unlike normal memory (Kihlstrom & Wilson, 1984). However, in accordance with the non-state position, similar disorganization effects can be shown by subjects who have been instructed to "pretend to forget", or to "attend away" from the material (Spanos, 1986a; Wagstaff, 1982). It has also been proposed that "reals" and simulators differ in the extent to which they show "source amnesia"; that is, after a session of hypnosis, unlike simulators, "reals" will sometimes recall information given to them when they were "hypnotized", but they say they cannot remember where they learned this information (Evans, 1979). However, Wagstaff (1981) suggests that one reason why simulators may fail to show source amnesia is that, in trying to be excellent subjects, they show total amnesia, that is, amnesia for both the information to be recalled and the source. Later studies have supported this interpretation and have shown that non-hypnotic task-motivated subjects and simulators instructed to show partial amnesia also display source amnesia (Coe, 1989).

Nevertheless, state theorists remain unconvinced that the mechanisms proposed by non-state theorists can account adequately for hypnotic amnesia (see, e.g., Bowers & Davidson, 1991), so this debate will continue.

HYPNOTIC ANALGESIA

On first consideration, the fact that hypnosis can enable patients to endure surgery with little or no pain (hypnotic analgesia) might seem incompatible with a non-state viewpoint, and a number of theorists adhere to this opinion. However, non-state theorists insist that it is possible to explain hypnotic analgesia in terms of "ordinary" psychological processes, and argue the following: first, cases of surgery with hypnosis alone are rare, and some individuals can tolerate pain without medication or hypnosis; second, much major surgery is actually less painful than is commonly expected; and third, pain is a complex sensation that can be alleviated through relaxation, the reduction of stress and anxiety, and the use of strategies such as distraction and the reinterpretation of noxious stimulation; all of which are frequently involved in cases of hypnotic surgery (Chaves, 1989; Spanos & Chaves, 1989).

Because of the difficulties involved in the interpretation of clinical cases researchers have turned to laboratory studies of pain in an attempt to test the state and non-state explanations of hypnotic analgesia. In these studies pain is most usually induced by plunging the subject's hand into ice cold water, or applying a pressure stimulus. According to state theorists, laboratory studies show that suggestions for analgesia can be more effective when given in the hypnotic state than in the "waking" state (Hilgard, 1986; Hilgard & Hilgard, 1983). However, non-state theorists point to the fact that many of the studies supportive of this view have tended to use the same subjects in both the hypnotic and non-hypnotic conditions and are thus vulnerable to the criticism that, to fulfil the demands of the experimental situation, subjects may not have used pain-reducing and coping strategies in the non-hypnotic situation; in some cases, subjects may even have faked an absence of pain in the hypnotic situation (Wagstaff, 1981). In support of this interpretation, Spanos and his associates report that hypnotic analgesia is more, less, or equally as effective as non-hypnotic analgesia, depending on the expectations conveyed to the subjects; moreover, for subjects who are not hypnotically susceptible, hypnotic suggestions seem to be less effective than other pain-reducing strategies, such as distraction (Spanos, 1986a, 1989). Nevertheless, some state theorists continue to report that hypnotic suggestions for analgesia are superior to non-hypnotic interventions (Bowers & Davidson, 1991).

Some of the most interesting results on hypnotic analgesia have come from "hidden observer" reports. Hilgard (1986) found that, following suggestions for analgesia, hypnotic subjects typically report pain relief; however, when the "hidden observer" is contacted (by placing a hand on the subject's shoulder), the "hidden part" reports higher levels of pain only slightly less than those reported in the normal "waking" state. Hilgard argues that this occurs because pain *is* experienced during hypnotic analgesia, but the "part" experiencing pain is dissociated from awareness by an "amnesic barrier". In contrast, non-state theorists argue that the reports of the "hidden observer" simply reflect what subjects think they are expected to say as implied by the experimental instructions (Spanos, 1989; Wagstaff, 1981).

Not surprisingly Hilgard's supporters disagree with the view that one can explain his finding solely in terms of subjects reporting what they think they ought to report. For example, Nogrady et al. (1983) found that if "reals" and simulators are given only a hint that higher pain reports are expected from the "hidden observer", then some "reals" show the classic "hidden observer" effect, where as no simulators show it. But in reply, Spanos, Gywnn, and Stam (1983) argue that the reason why the simulators had failed in this study to respond like the "reals" was because, trying to act like excellent subjects and not give themselves, away, they had acted conservatively in the face of ambiguous instructions; so, to test this idea further, they ran a study in which they removed the subtle hint for higher pain reports from the "hidden observer"; as they predicted, the standard "hidden observer" effect was then virtually eliminated. Spanos (1989) argue, that this latter finding is inconsistent with the view that hypnotic analgesia occurs because the actual pain is "held" in a separate cognitive subsystem behind an amnesic barrier. To add further support for the non-state view, Spanos and his associates have found that "hidden observers" will report greater, the same, or less pain than the ordinary "hypnotized" part, if these expectations are conveyed to them (Spanos, 1989).

Also somewhat disquieting to the state view of hypnotic analgesia is apparent support for Wagstaff's (1981, 1991) contention that reports of hypnotic analgesia may be inflated by compliance or faking. Thus Spanos, Perlini, Patrick, Bell, and Gwynn (1990) found that, if *after* receiving a painful stimulus, it is implied to hypnotic subjects that they were, or were not, "hypnotized" at the time they were experiencing the stimulus, they will report pain relief, or not, accordingly.

Disagreements about the mechanisms involved in hypnotic pain control are as rife as ever, but perhaps the most fascinating outcome of research in this area is the realization that human beings have a considerable capacity to control and tolerate pain without chemical analgesics.

CLINICAL HYPNOSIS

There is little doubt that hypnotic techniques have been used successfully in the clinical field for the treatment of many problems other than pain. For example, successful outcomes have been reported in the treatment of problems such as insomnia, obesity, mild phobias, smoking, and dental stress (Heap & Dryden, 1991; Wadden & Anderton, 1982). However, once again, difficulties arise in deciding whether it is necessary to postulate an "hypnotic state" to explain such effects. Hypnotic techniques typically involve a variety of factors that are not unique to hypnosis, and could account for the improvements; these include social support, relaxation, covert modelling, and even social compliance (Wadden & Anderton, 1982; Wagstaff, 1981). A number of claims have been made that hypnosis may be useful in the treatment of physical symptoms such as skin problems and even cancer. Unfortunately it seems that, as yet, research in these areas has not been sufficiently rigorous to isolate the factors involved in treatment success, or, in some cases, to decide even whether the treatment was successful (Johnson, 1989; Stam, 1989).

Clearly, regardless, of whether one believes in the notion of an hypnotic state, the area of clinical hypnosis remains a rich source of data on the psychological influences on physical illness, and one that should bear fruit as research into hypnosis continues.

HYPNOTIC SUSCEPTIBILITY

Are some people more susceptible to hypnotic suggestions than others; if so, why? Research indicates that people differ widely in their susceptibility to hypnotic suggestions; but state and non-state theorists tend to differ in their explanations of these differences. Various attempt have been made to relate hypnotic susceptibility to a number of physiological and performance parameters including attentional skills, EEG activity, right brain hemisphere processing, and eye movements, but, on the whole, such attempts have been inconclusive (Spanos, 1982). In contrast, both state and non-state theorists seem to agree that the tendency to become absorbed in imaginings is one of the main correlates of hypnotic susceptibility. However, they differ in their interpretations of this finding. According to state theorists, the reason why this relationship occurs is because absorption in imaginings may reflect a capacity to dissociate, and at the heart of hypnotic responding is the capacity for dissociation (see, e.g., Bowers, 1983). Non-state theorists argue that it would not be surprising if a propensity to fantasize and become involved in imaginings should correlate with hypnotic susceptibility as this would facilitate the enactment of the role of the "hypnotized" individual, but they do not see why this relationship should be viewed as evidence for differences in the ability to enter an altered state of consciousness.

Non-state theorists also argue that there are a number of other factors that have been found to correlate with hypnotic susceptibility and can be seen as supportive of their view; these include social conformity, acting or drama skills, and possessing appropriate attitudes and expectancies (Spanos, 1986b; Wagstaff, 1986, 1991). Indeed, if hypnotic susceptibility is seen as not a fixed ability or trait, but a strategic response to a particular context, then by modifying subjects' attitudes and expectancies, and training them how to use their imaginations to pass suggestions, it should be possible to change "low" hypnotic responders into "highs". This is exactly what Spanos and his colleagues have claimed to have done (Bertrand, 1989). However, critics have argued that such training techniques may encourage subjects to fake rather than evoke genuine changes in hypnotic susceptibility (Bowers & Davidson, 1991).

CONCLUSION

Research and debate in hypnosis obviously flourishes, but in over one hundred years we seem to be no further forward in deciding whether there is an altered state of consciousness that we can call "hypnosis". However, the lessons that this controversy has taught us are many. We have accumulated valuable knowledge about the problems associated with experiments on human beings, lessons valuable not only to psychology but also to other disciplines, and we have learned much about the capacities and vulnerabilities of ordinary people.

Traditionally, it seems that hypnosis has almost been viewed as an embarrassment to psychologists – something better left to psychiatrists or parapsychologists. However, the high standard of research in this area makes such a view untenable; perhaps now is the time for the topic of hypnosis to be placed firmly where it belongs, on the mainstream psychology syllabus.

FURTHER READING

Bowers, K. S. (1983). *Hypnosis for the seriously curious.* New York: Norton.

Hilgard, E. R. (1986). *Divided consciousness: Multiple controls in human thought and action* (expanded edn). New York: Wiley.

Lynn, S. J., & Rhue, J. W. (Eds) (1991). *Theories of hypnosis: Current models and perspectives.* New York: Guilford.

Spanos, N. P. (1986). Hypnotic behavior: A social psychological interpretation of amnesia, analgesia and trance logic. *Behavioral and Brain Sciences, 9,* 449–467.

Spanos, N. P., & Chaves, J. F. (Eds) (1989). *Hypnosis: The cognitive-behavioral perspective.* Buffalo, NY: Prometheus.

REFERENCES

Barber, J. (1991). The locksmith model: Accessing hypnotic responsiveness. In S. J. Lynn & J. W. Rhue (Eds) *Theories of hypnosis: Current models and perspectives* (pp. 241–274). New York: Guilford.

Barber, T. X. (1969). *Hypnosis: A scientific approach.* New York: Van Nostrand.

Barber, T. X., Spanos, N. P., & Chaves, J. F. (1974). *Hypnosis, imagination, and human potentialities.* Elmsford, NY: Pergamon.

Bertrand, L. D. (1989). The assessment and modification of hypnotic susceptibility. In N. P. Spanos & J. F. Chaves (Eds) *Hypnosis: The cognitive-behavioral perspective* (pp. 18–31). Buffalo, NY: Prometheus.

Bowers, K. S. (1983). *Hypnosis for the seriously curious.* New York: Norton.

Bowers, K. S., & Davidson, T. M. (1991). A neo-dissociative critique of Spanos's Social-Psychological model of hypnosis. In S. J. Lynn & J. W. Rhue (Eds) *Theories of hypnosis: Current models and perspectives* (pp. 105–143). New York: Guilford.

Chaves, J. F. (1989). Hypnotic control of clinical pain. In N. P. Spanos & J. F. Chaves (Eds) *Hypnosis: The cognitive-behavioral perspective* (pp. 242–271). Buffalo, NY: Prometheus.

Coe, W. C. (1989). Post-hypnotic amnesia. Theory and research. In N. P. Spanos & J. F. Chaves (Eds) *Hypnosis: The cognitive-behavioral perspective* (pp. 110–148). Buffalo, NY: Prometheus.

de Groot, H. P. & Gwynn, M. I. (1989). Trance logic, duality, and hidden-observer responding. In N. P. Spanos & J. F. Chaves (Eds) *Hypnosis: The cognitive-behavioral perspective* (pp. 187–205). Buffalo, NY: Prometheus.

Edmonston, W. E. (1991). Anesis. In S. J. Lynn & J. W. Rhue (Eds) *Theories of hypnosis: Current models and perspectives* (pp. 197–240). New York: Guilford.

Evans, F. J. (1979). Contextual forgetting: Post-hypnotic source amnesia. *Journal of Abnormal Psychology, 88,* 556–563.

Fellows, B. J. (1990). Current theories of hypnosis: A critical overview. *British Journal of Experimental and Clinical Hypnosis, 7,* 81–92.

Gravitz, M. A., & Gerton, M. I. (1984). Origins of the term hypnotism prior to Braid. *American Journal of Clinical Hypnosis, 27,* 107–110.

Gruzelier, J. (1988). The neuropsychology of hypnosis. In M. Heap (Ed.) *Hypnosis: Current clinical, experimental and forensic practices* (pp. 68–76). London: Croom Helm.

Heap, M., & Dryden, W. (1991). *Hypnotherapy: A handbook*. Milton Keynes: Open University Press.

Hilgard, E. R. (1986). *Divided consciousness: Multiple controls in human thought and action* (expanded edn). New York: Wiley.

Hilgard, E. R. (1991). A neodissociation interpretation of hypnosis. In S. J. Lynn & J. W. Rhue (Eds) *Theories of hypnosis: Current models and perspectives* (pp. 83–104). New York: Guilford.

Hilgard, E. R., & Hilgard, J. R. (1983). *Hypnosis in the relief of pain*. Los Altos, CA: Wiulliam Kaufmann.

Jacobs, S., & Gotthelf, C. (1986). Effects of hypnosis on physical and athletic performance. In F. A. De Piano & H. C. Salzberg (Eds) *Clinical applications of hypnosis* (pp. 157–173). Norwood, NJ: Ablex.

Johnson, R. F. Q. (1989). Hypnosis, suggestion, and dermatological changes: A consideration of the production and diminution of dermatological entities. In N. P. Spanos & J. F. Chaves (Eds) *Hypnosis: The cognitive-behavioral perspective* (pp. 297–312). Buffalo, NY: Prometheus.

Jones, W. J., & Flynn, D. M. (1989). Methodological and theoretical considerations in the study of "hypnotic" effects in perception. In N. P. Spanos & J. F. Chaves (Eds) *Hypnosis: The cognitive-behavioral perspective* (pp. 149–174). Buffalo, NY: Prometheus.

Kihlstrom, J. F., & Wilson, L. (1984). Temporal organization of recall during posthypnotic amnesia. *Journal of Abnormal Psychology*, *93*, 200–208.

Kihlstrom, J. F., Evans, F. J., Orne, E. C., & Orne, M. T. (1980). Attempting to breach posthypnotic amnesia. *Journal of Abnormal Psychology*, *89*, 603–616.

Knox, J. V., Morgan, A. H., & Hilgard, E. R. (1974). Pain and suffering in ischemia: The paradox of hypnotically suggested anesthesia as contradicted by reports from the "hidden-observer". *Archives of General Psychiatry*, *30*, 840–847.

Malott, J. M. (1984). Active-alert hypnosis. Replication and extension of previous research. *Journal of Abnormal Psychology*, *93*, 246–249.

Nogrady, H., McConkey, K. M., Laurence, J. R., & Perry, C. (1983). Dissociation, duality, and demand characteristics in hypnosis. *Journal of Abnormal Psychology*, *92*, 223–235.

Obstoj, J., & Sheehan, P. W. (1977). Aptitude for trance, task generalizability and incongruity response in hypnosis. *Journal of Abnormal Psychology*, *86*, 543–552.

Orne, M. T. (1959). The nature of hypnosis: Artifact and essence. *Journal of Abnormal and Social Psychology*, *58*, 277–299.

Orne, M. T. (1966). Hypnosis, motivation and compliance. *American Journal of Psychiatry*, *122*, 721–726.

Orne, M. T. (1979). On the simulating subject as quasi-control group in hypnosis research: what, why, and how? In E. Fromm & R. E. Shor (Eds) *Hypnosis: Research developments and perspectives* (pp. 519–565). New York: Aldine.

Orne, M. T., Sheehan, P. W., & Evans, F. J. (1968). The occurrence of posthypnotic behavior outside the experimental setting. *Journal of Personality and Social Psychology*, *26*, 217–221.

Sarbin, T. R., & Coe, W. C. (1972). *Hypnosis: A social psychological analysis of influence communication*. New York: Holt, Rinehart & Winston.

Spanos, N. P. (1982). A social psychological approach to hypnotic behavior. In G. Weary & H. L. Mirels (Eds) *Integrations of clinical and social psychology* (pp. 231–271). New York: Oxford University Press.

Spanos, N. P. (1986a). Hypnotic behavior: A social psychological interpretation of amnesia, analgesia and trance logic. *Behavioral and Brain Sciences, 9,* 449–467.

Spanos, N. P. (1986b). Hypnosis and the modification of hypnotic susceptibility: A social psychological perspective. In P. L. N. Naish (Ed.) *What is hypnosis?* (pp. 85–120). Philadelphia, PA: Open University Press.

Spanos, N. P. (1989). Experimental research on hypnotic analgesia. In N. P. Spanos & J. F. Chaves (Eds) *Hypnosis: The cognitive-behavioral perspective* (pp. 206–241). Buffalo, NY: Prometheus.

Spanos, N. P. (1991). A sociocognitive approach to hypnosis. In S. J. Lynn & J. W. Rhue (Eds) *Theories of hypnosis: Current models and perspectives* (pp. 324–362). New York: Guilford.

Spanos, N. P., & Chaves, J. F. (1989). Hypnotic analgesia and surgery: In defence of the social-psychological position. *British Journal of Experimental and Clinical Hypnosis, 6,* 131–139.

Spanos, N. P., Gwynn, M. I., & Stam, H. J. (1983). Instructional demands and ratings of overt and hidden pain during hypnotic analgesia. *Journal of Abnormal Psychology, 92,* 479–488.

Spanos, N. P., de Groot, H. P., Tiller, D. K., Weekes, J. R., & Bertrand, L. D. (1985). "Trance logic" duality and hidden observer responding in hypnotic, imagination control and simulating subjects. *Journal of Abnormal Psychology, 94,* 611–623.

Spanos, N. P., Menary, E., Brett, P. J., Cross, W., & Ahmed, Q. (1987). Failure of posthypnotic responding to occur outside the experimental setting. *Journal of Abnormal Psychology, 96,* 52–57.

Spanos, N. P., Perlini, A. H., Patrick, L., Bell, S., & Gwynn, M. I. (1990). The role of compliance in hypnotic and nonhypnotic analgesia. *Journal of Research in Personality, 24,* 433–453.

Stam, H. J. (1989). From symptom relief to cure. Hypnotic interventions in cancer. In N. P. Spanos & J. F. Chaves (Eds) *Hypnosis: The cognitive-behavioral perspective* (pp. 313–339). Buffalo, NY: Prometheus.

Wadden, T., & Anderton, C. H. (1982). The clinical use of hypnosis. *Psychological Bulletin, 91,* 215–243.

Wagstaff, G. F. (1977). An experimental study of compliance and post-hypnotic amnesia. *British Journal of Social and Clinical Psychology, 16,* 225–228.

Wagstaff, G. F. (1981). *Hypnosis, compliance, and belief.* Brighton: Harvester.

Wagstaff, G. F. (1982). Disorganized recall, suggested amnesia, and compliance. *Psychological Reports, 51,* 1255–1258.

Wagstaff, G. F. (1989). Forensic aspects of hypnosis. In N. P. Spanos & J. F. Chaves (Eds) *Hypnosis: The cognitive-behavioral perspective* (pp. 340–359). Buffalo, NY: Prometheus.

Wagstaff, G. F. (1991). Compliance, belief and semantics in hypnosis: A non-state sociocognitive perspective. In S. J. Lynn & J. W. Rhue (Eds) *Theories of hypnosis: Current models and perspectives* (pp. 362–396). New York: Guilford.

Zamansky, H. S., & Bartis, S. P. (1985). The dissociation of an experience: The hidden observer observed. *Journal of Abnormal Psychology, 94,* 243–248.

3

GENDER ISSUES IN PSYCHOLOGY

Mary Crawford
University of South Carolina, Pennsylvania, USA
Rhoda K. Unger
Montclair State College, New Jersey, USA

Since the late 1960s, scholars and practitioners in psychology have engaged in sustained evaluation of the discipline's representation of women and gender. This critique has developed in a social context of changing roles and opportunities for women and the emergence of a feminist social movement.

Of course, the women's movement originating in the late 1960s was not the first. A previous women's rights initiative had reached its peak over a hundred years earlier. At the turn of the century, many of the first generation of scientifically trained women psychologists, perhaps influenced by the earlier movement, devoted their research efforts to examining accepted wisdom about the extent and nature of sex differences. Determined to demonstrate women's capacity to contribute to science on an equal basis with men, they laboured to refute hypotheses that they themselves did not find credible and that they did not believe could account for the inferior social position of women (Unger, 1979). While some achieved a measure of professional success, as group they succeeded neither in legitimizing nor institutionalizing the study of women and gender (Rosenberg 1982; Scarborough & Furumoto, 1987).

Psychology's interest in sex differences and gender waned with the rise of behaviourism. Gender would not return to the research agenda until the 1970s, and it was only in the mid-1980s that an *Annual Review of Psychology* article could state that it was an idea whose time had come (Deaux, 1985). As psychologists have once again begun to examine psychology's understandings of women, problems and inadequacies have been catalogued:

> There was widespread agreement about [psychology's] faults: that women were infrequently studied; that theories were constructed from a male-as-normative viewpoint and that women's behavior was explained as deviation from the male standard; that the stereotype of women was considered an accurate portrayal of women's behavior; that women who fulfilled the dictates of the gender stereotype were viewed as healthy and happy; that differences in the behaviors of women and men were attributed to differences in anatomy and physiology; and that the social context which often shapes behavior was ignored in the case of women. (Kahn & Jean, 1983, p. 660)

Unlike its earlier counterpart, the new psychology of women and gender has become institutionalized. Before 1968, there were virtually no psychology departments offering courses in the psychology of women and/or gender; in the early 1990s about half of all US psychology departments provided them. Psychology of women courses are often connected to, and have contributed to, the rapid growth of women's studies programmes, which in the 1990s exist on over 450 US college and university campuses (Stimpson, 1986). The new field has its own journals, which are important resources for scholars and students: *Sex Roles*, which began publishing in 1975, *Psychology of Women Quarterly*, since 1977, and *Feminism & Psychology*, a UK addition in 1991.

Women psychologists and men who support their goals have worked toward an improved status for women within psychology. They first formed the Association for Women in Psychology (AWP) in 1969, then lobbied the American Psychological Association (APA) to form a division of the Psychology of Women. This division, officially approved in 1973, is now one of the larger divisions of the APA, with over 3,000 members. A similar pattern of progress in incorporating women occurred among Canadian psychologists, and (more recently) within the British Psychological Society. These organizational changes have acknowledged the presence of women in psychology and helped enhance their professional identity (O'Connell & Russo, 1991; Scarborough & Furumoto, 1987).

The new psychology of women and gender is rich and varied. Virtually every intellectual framework from Freudian theory to cognitive psychology has been used in developing new theories and approaches. Virtually every area of psychology, from developmental to social, has been affected (Crawford & Marecek, 1989). In this chapter we shall examine first some conceptual and methodological issues, and then provide reviews of selected research topics. Throughout, we shall note connections to clinical/practice issues.

CONCEPTUAL AND METHODOLOGICAL ISSUES

Gender: more than just sex

Feminist psychology makes a conceptual distinction between sex and gender (Unger, 1979). *Sex* is defined as biological differences in genetic composition and reproductive anatomy and function. *Gender* is what culture makes out of the "raw material" of biological sex. All known societies recognize biological differentiation and use it as the basis for social distinctions. In North American society, the process of creating gendered human beings starts at birth. When a baby is born, the presence of a vagina or penis represents sex – but the pink or blue blanket that soon enfolds the baby represents gender. The blanket serves as a cue that this infant is to be treated as girl or boy, not as a "generic human", from the start.

The influence of gender-based social distinctions is pervasive. Gender-related processes influence behaviour, thoughts, and feelings in individuals; they affect interactions among individuals; and they help determine the structure of social institutions. The processes by which differences are created and power is allocated can be understood by considering how gender is played out at three levels: societal, interpersonal, and individual.

The social structural level: gender as a system of power relations

In the broadest sense, gender is a classification system that shapes the relations among women and men. For example, virtually all societies label some tasks as "men's" and others as "women's" work. While there is a great deal of variability in tasks assigned to each sex across societies, whatever is labelled "women's work" is usually seen as less important and desirable. Not only women's work but also women themselves are devalued. Thus gender can be viewed as a system of social classification that influences access to power and resources (Crawford & Marecek, 1989; Sherif, 1982).

39

The interpersonal level: gender as a cue

In every society, certain traits, behaviours, and interests are associated with each sex and assumed to be appropriate for people of that sex. Since there are only two sexes, gender is also assumed to be dichotomous: a person can be classified as either "masculine" or "feminine", but not both. Although many traits, interests, behaviours, and even physical characteristics are ascribed to women *or* men, in reality, people often show characteristics ascribed to the other sex. Thus gender, as it is usually framed, reflects a form of stereotyping (Deaux & Major, 1987; Unger & Crawford, 1992).

Gender stereotypes are brought to bear in social interaction, where the influence of sex and gender interact. Not only do people use gender cues to make inferences about sex, but also they use perceived sex to make inferences about gender. Gender cues are used to tell us how to behave towards others in social interactions. Although much sex-differential treatment happens outside awareness, research confirms its occurrence. For example, observations in elementary or primary school classrooms show that, although teachers believe that they are treating boys and girls the same, boys receive more attention, both positive and negative, than girls do. Boys are yelled at and criticized more in front of their classmates. Moreover, in some classes, a few boys are allowed to dominate class time by interacting constantly with the teacher, while most students remain silent (Eccles, 1989).

Research shows that the behaviour of men and boys is often evaluated more positively than the behaviour of women and girls. Even when a woman and a man behave in identical ways, their behaviour may be interpreted differently (Porter & Geis, 1981; Wallstrom & O'Leary, 1981; Wiley & Eskilson, 1982; Yarkin, Town, & Wallston, 1982). Moreover, sexual categorization is not only a way of seeing differences, but also a way of creating differences. When men and women are treated differently in ordinary daily interactions, they may come to behave differently in return. These processes will be discussed later (see below, "Doing gender").

The individual level: gender as masculinity and femininity

To a greater or lesser extent, women and men come to accept gender distinctions visible at the structural level and enacted at the interpersonal level as part of the self-concept. They become *gender-typed*, ascribing to themselves the traits, behaviours, and roles normative for people of their sex in their culture. Women, moreover, internalize their devaluation and subordination. Feminist theories of personality development (e.g., Miller, 1986) stress that "feminine" characteristics such as passivity, excessive concern with pleasing others, lack of initiative, and dependency are psychological consequences of subordination. Members of subordinate social groups who adopt such characteristics are considered well adjusted; those who do not are controlled by psychiatric diagnosis, violence or the threat of violence, and social ostracism.

Much of the psychology of women and gender has consisted of documenting the effects of internalized subordination. Laboratory and field research, as well as clinical experience, attest that, compared to boys and men, girls and women lack a sense of personal entitlement (Apfelbaum, 1986; Major, McFarlin, & Gagnon, 1984), pay themselves less for comparable work (Major & Deaux, 1982), are equally satisfied with their employment, even though they are paid significantly less than men (Crosby, 1982), lose self-esteem and confidence in their academic ability, especially in mathematics and science, as they progress through the educational system (Chipman & Wilson, 1985; Eccles (Parsons) et al., 1985), and are more likely to suffer from disturbances of body image, eating disorders, and depression (McGrath, Keita, Strickland, & Russo, 1990; McCauley, Mintz, & Glenn, 1988; Hesse-Biber, 1989).

Gender at the social structural level has traditionally been the province of sociology and anthropology, while the interactional level has been encompassed by social psychology and the individual level by clinical, developmental, and personality psychology. In studying women and gender it is necessary to focus on one level while keeping sight of the system as a whole. Just as clinicians who treat the effects of internalized subordination must conceptualize and respond to structural aspects of clients' problems (Greenspan, 1983), researchers in the psychology of gender must place their work in the context of gendered social structures. Both clinicians and researchers share conceptual and methodological concerns with those attempting to understand other systems of social classification such as age, "race", and class (Brown & Root, 1990).

Methodological innovations and epistemological debates

The psychology of women and gender has generated substantial critique of psychology's traditional methods of research; selection of research participants has been a major area of contention. Many feminist researchers have examined the biases produced by ignoring the sex of the participants, by studying men more than women, and/or by examining one sex more than the other in certain situational contexts, such as affiliation among women or aggressiveness among men (cf. Grady, 1981; McHugh, Koeske, & Frieze, 1986; Wallston & Grady, 1985).

Feminist researchers have also raised similar questions about the exclusion of race and ethnicity, social class, and sexual orientation (Denmark, Russo, Frieze, & Sechzer, 1988). This kind of exclusion may lead to overgeneralizations about women as a global category similar to earlier overgeneralizations about human beings based largely on studies of men.

Others have raised more basic questions about the way research questions are generated and the values reflected by the way questions are asked. For example, much research has focused on whether mothers' outside employment endangers their children's psychological welfare. There is much less research, however, on whether fathers' work commitments harm their children or whether mothers' employment might be beneficial (Hare-Mustin & Marecek, 1990). Similar questions have been raised about comparison groups in psychological research; for example, when a biomedical study includes both sexes, should the two samples be matched on physical or social criteria (Parlee, 1981)?

The most intense debates in the area of research methodology have been about whether and how to conduct research on sex differences (cf., Unger, 1979, 1990; Unger & Crawford, 1992, chap. 3). Issues raised include whether researchers should stress similarities rather than differences since every psychological trait studied shows large overlaps between females and males; confusions between description and explanation; and problems associated with using biological rather than social explanations for the differences found. Despite cogent criticisms of specific problems in this kind of research (cf. Jacklin, 1981), dubious practices continue. Researchers using meta-analysis have questioned the stability and permanence of so-called sex differences (Hyde & Linn, 1986).

Despite the critiques, few methodological alternatives have emerged thus far (Fine & Gordon, 1989). Peplau and Conrad (1989) have examined feminist methodological issues and concluded that all methods can be used or abused. Thus, while the experimental method not only is inherently hierarchical, can result in context stripping and may be ecologically invalid, it can on the other hand result in the elucidation of psychological mechanisms that are difficult to detect in a normal environment. Similarly, so-called feminine qualitative methodology can be used for or against women. For example, Freud used qualitative methodology, but has frequently been accused of an anti-female bias.

One of the great innovations in feminist research has been to make values and politics explicit. Personal experience sensitizes people to different aspects of problems. Because the values of dominant groups in society are normative, they are not always recognized as values. When others – women or minorities, for example – question the assumptions of the dominant group, the underlying values are made more visible (Unger, 1983).

Using innovative techniques, some feminist researchers have explored value contradictions between groups of women. For example, Fine (1983–1984) showed how white middle-class assumptions about effective coping following a rape may not be helpful for poor black women. Lykes (1989) found that her use of a written signed consent form was seen as a violation of personal trust by the Guatemalan Indian women with whom she worked. Feminist clinicians have explored how similarities and differences in group membership and values between therapist and client can affect the course of therapy (Lerman & Porter, 1990).

The psychology of women and gender is not unique in being influenced by societal factors. Values and beliefs about the way the world works have been found to be related more to political and religious identity than to sex (Unger, 1992). These data question theories that stress a unique female epistemology or moral orientation. Feminist theorists have also argued that values and beliefs help to create reality rather than simply bias what aspects of reality we perceive (cf., Hare-Mustin & Marecek, 1990). Evidence for the social construction of reality has been provided by mainstream cognitive researchers as well as by feminists (Unger & Crawford, 1992).

Because psychology is part of our culture, doing psychological research is inevitably a political act (Crawford & Marecek, 1989). Feminist research is, therefore, explicitly political. It is particularly concerned with the impact of differential distinctions on individuals who regularly receive lower evaluations because of their social category. The topics in this chapter were chosen partially because they illuminate such phenomena as well as being representative of current research and practice in the field.

GENDER AND DEVELOPMENT THROUGH THE LIFESPAN

The area of gender development has been of great interest to psychologists for many years. Attention has now shifted away from concern with the socialization of gender in childhood to more interactive lifespan perspectives. According to such interactive models of social development, gender-related perceptions and behaviours change throughout the lifespan both because society's demands change with people's age and because people interpret seemingly identical messages about gender differently as they mature.

Childhood: becoming gendered

Current research on childhood has continued to find evidence that gender-characteristic traits in children of both sexes are shaped by parental attitudes and behaviours. Data ranging from sex-selective abortion practices to behavioural observations of the treatment of newborn infants show that males remain the preferred sex (Unger & Crawford, 1992, chap. 7). Pressure for gender-role conformity is stronger for boys than girls at an earlier age. Differential parental treatment tends to produce gender stereotypic traits of independence and efficacy in boys and emotional sensitivity, nurturance, and helplessness in girls. Parents appear largely unaware that they treat daughters and sons differently.

Children are not merely the passive recipients of gender socialization but active participants in it. By the nursery school years, girls and boys have different preferences in play and toys (Maccoby, 1988). In this age group, the choice of toy determines the sex of one's playmates rather than the other way around (Roopnarine, 1984). By the primary school years, girls and boys have formed sex-segregated social networks based on these preferences (Maccoby, 1988). Such sex segregation is greatest in situations that have *not* been structured by adults.

Sex segregation persists until adolescence, maintained by social control mechanisms such as teasing (Thorne & Luria, 1986). In same-sex peer interaction, boys and girls learn different styles of social influence and norms for aggression. These gender-characteristic patterns are not equally effective in mixed sex groups. For example, the physical dominance tactics used by boys to influence each other appear to be more effective in mixed sex situations than are the verbal persuasion techniques more frequently used by girls (Charlesworth & Dzur, 1987).

As children acquire cultural norms for stereotyping they become more intolerant of peers who deviate from these norms (Carter & McCloskey, 1984). Pressure for conformity is stronger for boys than for girls, as a quick scrutiny of the differential connotations of "tomboy" versus "sissy" easily demonstrates. Ironically, girls and women are probably permitted more latitude because boys and men are seen as the more valuable sex and, thus, as requiring greater attention to their socialization.

Short-term interventions designed by adults to help children unlearn gender typing are relatively ineffective because of peer pressures (Carpenter, Huston, & Holt, 1986). However, some girls resist gender typing and actively participate in sports, mathematics, and science. Familial factors related to this type of positive social deviance include active parental encouragement and the absence of brothers. Social class and "racial" differences are also important, but require further investigation.

Puberty and adolescence: gendered transitions

Puberty adds complexity to the processes underlying gender development. Biological, social, and cultural processes are interrelated in the transition from girlhood to womanhood. Researchers have moved beyond simple physiological mechanisms to explanations involving the social and cultural meaning of pubertal changes (cf., Brooks-Gunn, 1987; Martin, 1987; Ussher, 1989).

A major area of attention is the social implications of increasing bodily differences between boys and girls. Probably because of the subjective meaning of bodily change, puberty appears to be a more difficult transition for girls than for boys. For example, puberty involves a greater increase in body fat composition for girls than for boys (who gain muscle mass). Western society has, however, developed increasingly stringent norms for thinness in women (Silverstein, Perdue, Peterson, & Kelley, 1986). Girls' dissatisfaction with their looks begins during puberty, along with a decline in self-esteem.

Comparisons between early- and late-maturing girls indicate that dissatisfaction with one's looks is associated with the rapid and normal weight gain that is part of growing up (Attie & Brooks-Gunn, 1989). In comparison to late-maturing girls, early-maturing girls have less positive body images despite the fact that they date more. This seeming paradox highlights the contradictions produced by the differential meaning of mature physical development in females as compared to males. An attractive appearance is stressed more for young women than men despite the fact that excessive thinness is physiologically more abnormal for them. Sexual activity is also more problematic for women than men because of still existing double standards and differential responsibility in the event of pregnancy. In contrast, physical maturation in males carries with it unambiguous social advantages including opportunities for enhanced athletic prowess, leadership roles, and expectations for occupational success (Unger & Crawford, 1992).

Research on puberty has also focused on differences within groups of women; this research indicates that causal effects should be looked for at the level of physiological and social interactions. But, it also suggests that ignoring cultural norms such as the meaning of physical appearance may lead to the omission of important explanatory variables. For example, studies of ethnicity and the development of eating disorders among young women suggest that women of colour have a lower risk of anorexia nervosa and bulimia nervosa than white women (Root, 1990). Ironically, women of colour may be protected from eating disorders because white standards of beauty are not applied to them and they are less subject to social demands for low body weight.

Social constructions of developmental events

Cross-racial and cross-cultural research on gender and development are particularly useful in disentangling physiological and social influences. It has been suggested, for example, that menstruation has different meanings for black and for white women (Martin, 1987). Similarly, menopause as a developmental transition seems to be associated with the status of ageing women in different cultures. The depressive symptoms associated with menopause in the United States do not appear to exist in non-western cultures where women gain status and political power as they age (Kaiser, 1990). These women are freed from taboos involving ideas about menstrual pollution, they gain seniority in their domestic unit, and they acquire new role opportunities. In contrast, images of ageing women in the USA are almost uniformly negative (Kimmel, 1988).

Research on reproductive events unique to women – such as pregnancy and childbirth, menarche and menstruation, and menopause – emphasizes the social construction of meaning around these normal developmental processes. Normal events are medicalized and evoked as clinical diagnoses and explanations (cf. Ussher, 1989), and become reified in the official diagnostic manual (Hamilton & Gallant, 1988). This emphasis on physiological causality may have led previous researchers to ignore sociocultural context and exaggerate differences between women and men (Unger & Crawford, 1992). Newer research examining cross-cultural and intra-cultural differences among groups of women is valuable for setting the limits of biological explanation.

DOING GENDER

One of the most interesting areas of research is one that some psychologists and sociologists refer to as "doing gender" (Unger, 1988; West & Zimmerman, 1987). This kind of research focuses more on the interpersonal aspects of gender than its intra-psychic characteristics; it analyses the way cognitive categories based on sex as a social cue influence people's behaviour and elicit gender-characteristic patterns of interaction. Thus, it conceptualizes gender as a process through which social inequalities are created and maintained (Crawford & Marecek, 1989).

Sex is a salient social category. Distinctions based on the sex of target persons influence a wide variety of behaviours. For example, in remembering "who said what" in a conversation, people make more within-sex than between-sex errors. All women (or men) seem to "look alike". People also tend to minimize differences within groups and exaggerate differences between them. This process is particularly noticeable when individuals of that social category are present as a small minority. Under these conditions, their characteristics are seen as more stereotypic. Thus, people see women as more feminine and men as more masculine when there are few other members of their sex present in a group. Women and men do not differ in their tendency to categorize and make social judgements based on the sex of the minority group. Parallel effects have been found when "race", rather than sex, is the salient category (Taylor, Fiske, Etcoff, & Ruderman, 1978).

Other cognitive mechanisms are also influenced by the sex of stimulus persons. For example, people "remember" different (and stereotypic) information about the same individual based on her sexual (lesbian or heterosexual) or occupational (librarian or waitress) label (Snyder & Uranowitz, 1978). They evaluate the same material differently depending upon whether it is associated with a male, female, or ambiguously named person (Paludi & Strayer, 1985). Many researchers have found different causal attributions based on cues associated with gender (e.g., Wallston & O'Leary, 1981).

People also alter their self-presentation strategies to confirm others' gender-related expectations. For example, when women believed that they were to be interviewed by a male chauvinist rather than a non-sexist potential employer, they wore more frilly clothing, jewellery, and perfume to the interview. The process by which people act in a way that confirms other people'

46

expectations about them is known as a self-fulfilling prophecy (e.g., Towson, Zanna, & MacDonald, 1989).

Self-fulfilling prophecies have been found in areas associated with gender such as physical attractiveness and some personality traits. One of the most dramatic demonstrations of the way self-fulfilling prophecies contribute to the perpetuation of gender stereotypes is a study by Skrypnek and Snyder (1982). Unacquainted pairs of women and men were asked to negotiate a division of labour on a series of work-related tasks that differed in their gender-role connotations. Individuals in each pair were located in a different room and communicated by means of a signalling system. Although each male participant was actually interacting with a female partner, some of the men were told that they were interacting with a male, some with a female partner, and some were not informed about the sex of their partner. During the first part of the study, men were given the opportunity to make the choices. Men were more likely to choose the more masculine tasks when they believed their partner was a woman than when they believed she was a man or had no information about her sex. Their partners provided behavioural confirmation of their beliefs. "Males" chose more masculine tasks whereas "females" chose more feminine tasks. The sex of assignment influenced their behaviour more than their actual sex did. Even after their male partners no longer had the opportunity to control the negotiations, many of the women continued to maintain "gender-appropriate behaviours" – appropriate for the sex to which they had been assigned.

Many gender-typed social behaviours are associated with status and power differences. Henley (1977) pioneered the study of the relationship between non-verbal behaviours associated with status and the behaviours of women and men. In many aspects of non-verbal behaviour women behave in a manner similar to men with low status and power and are treated by others as if they possess such subordinate status. Females' politeness, smiling, emotional responsiveness, smaller personal space, less frequent initiation of touching, and greater frequency of being interrupted all reflect subordinate status.

Researchers have manipulated assigned roles or levels of achievement to see if the way men customarily behave toward women is due more to gender or status. They have found that both men and women who are assigned higher social roles (e.g., teacher rather than student) or greater power tend to display non-verbal behaviours that are considered more characteristic of males. They claim more personal space, touch their partners more, and visually dominate their partners more than do women and men who have been granted less status and power in the experimental setting (Dovidio, Ellyson, Keating, Heltman, & Brown, 1988; Leffler, Gillespie, & Conaty, 1982). Non-verbal cues connoting status and power are readily decoded, but both men and women appear reluctant to use such cues to confer leadership on women (Porter & Geis, 1981).

The use of "masculine" forms of power by women is associated with a variety of social sanctions. For example, in mixed-sex groups men are more influenced by a woman who speaks tentatively than one who speaks assertively (Carli, 1990). Women who use expert power are rated by experienced managers as far colder than men using identical power strategies (Wiley & Eskilson, 1982).

A number of studies have also found that women are expected to be less competent as well as less powerful in groups (Dion, 1985). These perceptions are difficult to change. One set of researchers could change perceptions about male superiority on spatial tasks only by rigging the situation so that the women performed significantly better than did the men (Pugh & Wahrman, 1983). However, even these higher-performing women never gained a meaningful advantage over their male partners.

People use gender to infer power and status. For example, when students were given no information (other than their sex) about a man or a woman who were trying to influence each other in either a bank or a supermarket setting, they assumed the man had higher status and would be more successful in his influence attempts. When, however, job titles such as bank vice-president and teller were added to denote relative status, students used titles rather than gender to predict compliance (Eagly & Wood, 1982).

Gender-linked assumptions about power and powerlessness influence not only beliefs and attitudes but also behavioural interactions. Dovidio and Gaertner (1983) have provided a clever demonstration of the behavioural consequences of upsetting the customary relationship between sex and status. Male and female college students interacted with a male or female confederate who was introduced either as their superior or subordinate and who was purportedly of higher or lower ability than themselves. The confederate then had an "accident" in which a container of pencils was knocked to the floor. Status but not ability influenced the extent to which women were helped, whereas ability, not status, influenced the extent to which men were helped. Both sexes helped high- and low-ability women equally, but helped high-ability men more often than low-ability men. They helped women supervisors less than women subordinates, but did not differentiate in their assistance to men based on their rank.

This study demonstrates how customary status/sex confounds are maintained. Individuals who deviated from traditional expectations were penalized by receiving less assistance from others. The researchers found a parallel effect when superiors and subordinates differed in "race" rather than sex. Participants did not appear to realize that sexism or racism played a role in their helping behaviour.

These studies indicate the way that behaviours associated with masculinity and femininity are constructed in our society. Differential inferences and expectations based on sex as a social category lead to gender-differentiated behaviours to which target individuals respond. These behavioural responses confirm gender-stereotypic belief patterns. What begins in the minds of individuals becomes social reality.

SEXUALITY AND RELATIONSHIPS IN SOCIOCULTURAL CONTEXT

The development of sexual identity, sexual norms and behaviours, and the dynamics of intimate relationships are of clinical and theoretical concern to researchers in women and gender. Although sexual behaviour takes place between individuals, it is learned about and interpreted in the context of cultural institutions. Sexuality, the most intimate aspect of the self and the most private of experiences, is shaped by a social order where issues of status, dominance, and power affect that which is personal (Travis, 1990). Sexual desire, like gender itself, is a social construct, developed within the individual in the context of a particular time in history, social class and ethnic group, religion, and prevailing set of gender roles (Foucault, 1978; Rubin, 1984).

The repertoire of sexual acts that is recognized by a particular social group, together with the rules or guidelines for expected behaviour, and the expected punishments for violating the rules, form the basis of sexual scripts (Laws & Schwartz, 1977). Sexual scripts can be thought of as schemas for sexual concepts and events. They represent both pre-formed ways of understanding and interpreting potentially sex-relevant situations, and plans for action that people bring to such situations. Sexual scripts for practices such as dating (Rose & Frieze, 1989) mesh with norms and laws that govern the institution of marriage (Blumstein & Schwartz, 1983).

Content, vehicles, and consequences of sexual scripts

Popular culture provides many agents for the learning of sexual scripts. These include advertising, television programming, popular magazines, sex manuals, and romance novels (Altman, 1984; Jackson, 1987; Radway, 1984; Signorielli, 1989; Soley & Kurzbard, 1986).

The content of prevailing scripts on sexuality and relationships is almost exclusively heterosexual, focuses on male agency and control, and perpetuates a double standard for sexual activity that allows males a greater variety of sexual behaviours and partners (Unger & Crawford, 1992, chap. 9). Girls and women are rarely presented as active sexual agents, whether the medium is school sex education materials (Fine, 1988), adult sex manuals (Altman, 1984; Jackson, 1987), rock videos, or genre novels (Radway, 1984). The cultural muting of female sexual desire and agency – the "missing discourse of desire" (Fine, 1988) – has been related to clinical sexual dysfunction in women (Radlove, 1983; Tevlin & Leiblum, 1983). The emphasis on male pleasure and control, and the resulting difficulties for women in asserting a claim to safer sex, have been implicated in the increasing rate of

HIV infection, especially among women of colour. Finally, acceptance of scripts which encode women as passive and coy and men as conquerors has been related to the use of coercion by males in date and acquaintance rape and dating abuse (Muehlenhard & Linton, 1987; Russell, 1984).

Another aspect of sexual scripts is that youth, slimness, and conventional female attractiveness are presented as central dimensions of the schema for femininity and sexual desirability. Enhancing attractiveness thus becomes a central way of enacting sexuality for many women (Chapkis, 1986; Freedman, 1986; Ussher, 1989).

Much research has analysed cultural pressures for slimness. The representation of standards of female beauty has become more restrictive in the second half of the twentieth century; for example, the ideal body shape has (literally) narrowed, and the weight of movie actresses and models in women's magazines has been declining since about 1950 (Garner, Garfinkel, Schwartz, & Thompson, 1980). Popular media encode the message that women should stay slim (ads for diet foods occur at a 63:1 ratio in women's vs men's magazines) while at the same time stressing preoccupation with food (ads for sweets and snacks occur at a 359:1 ratio) (Silverstein, Perdue, Peterson, Vogel, & Fantini, 1986). The negative evaluation of normal female bodily shape has been related to psychological distress, low self-esteem, and negative body image in women (Freedman, 1986; Jackson, Sullivan, & Rostker, 1988; Stake & Lauer, 1987; Ussher, 1989).

Many groups are marginalized by the prevailing discourse of sexuality: lesbian and bisexual women and homosexual men (Boston Lesbian Psychologies Collective, 1987), women of colour (Espin, 1986), older women (Bell, 1989), and people with disabilities (Fine & Asch, 1988).

Power and roles in intimate relationships

The study of power and roles in marriage has a long history in psychology and sociology. Marriages have been categorized as traditional, modern, egalitarian, dual-earner, or dual-career based on the allocation of authority, degree of role differentiation, patterns of shared activities, and economic contributions (Peplau & Gordon, 1985). In most marriages, husbands have greater power than wives, due to a variety of social factors (Blumstein & Schwartz, 1983; Steil & Weltman, 1991). Marital satisfaction is affected by power differentials and flucuates over the life cycle, with the child-rearing years least satisfying (Rhyne, 1981; Ruble, Fleming, Hackel, & Stangor, 1988; Steinberg & Silverberg, 1987). Increasingly, researchers are studying the interplay of roles (spouse, parent, and paid worker), ongoing role negotiation in both sexes, and committed relationships other than heterosexual marriage (e.g., Crosby, 1987). Although research on gay and lesbian couples is compromised by sampling biases, it suggests that equality is more likely in lesbian relationships than heterosexual marriage, and that satisfaction is related to many of the same variables (Blumstein & Schwartz, 1983; Peplau & Gordon, 1985).

Researchers are beginning to compare mixed-sex and same-sex couples in efforts to untangle individual-level gender-effects (e.g., socialized differences) from interactional (e.g., role expectations) and structural effects (e.g., greater male access to external resources such as money). An interesting example is research on influence strategies. Gender stereotypes are clear: women are believed to use indirect, manipulative strategies (sulking, crying, alleging insensitivity in the partner) and men are believed to use direct strategies (expressing anger, calling for a rational discussion). Dating partners report that they believe such stereotypes and also that their own behaviour is congruent with them (Kelley et al., 1978).

If influence strategies are due to childhood socialization for females to be more emotional and males more task-oriented, both partners in a lesbian couple should use tactics such as withdrawal and emotionality; among gay men, both partners should use more direct tactics. However, in a study of self-reported influence strategies in lesbians, gay men, and heterosexuals, sex affected the type of strategy employed only among the heterosexuals. In all groups, the individual who saw him/herself as the more powerful partner used direct, interactive strategies and the less-powerful partner used indirect and non-interactional tactics (Falbo & Peplau, 1980). Thus, "sex-related" strategies may be more accurately considered "power-related" strategies. This interpretation is supported by cross-cultural research showing that women from the United States use more direct influence tactics than women from Mexico, who have relatively less economic and social power (Belk, Garcia-Falconi, Hernandez-Sanchez, & Snell, 1988).

CONCLUSION

The new psychology of women and gender encompasses virtually every subfield within the discipline. The revisionist work of feminist psychologists holds the possibility of transforming the discipline into a true psychology of people. In addition to the selected topics reviewed here, there is a great deal of research on interactions of multiple roles such as spouse, parent, and worker; the causes, incidence, and effects of forms of violence against women; personality development across the lifespan; the psychology of pregnancy and mothering; masculinity and male roles; stereotypes; sexual differentiation, variation, and the social construction of sexual dichotomy; work and achievement. The volumes suggested below invite the reader to participate in the rich knowledge and ongoing debates of this emerging field.

FURTHER READING

Basow, S. A. (1992). *Gender stereotypes and roles* (3rd edn) Pacific Grove, CA: Brooks/Cole.

Crosby, F. (Ed.) (1987). *Spouse, parent, worker: On gender and multiple roles*. New Haven, CT: Yale University Press.

Hare-Mustin, R. T., & Marecek, J. (Eds) (1990). *Making a difference: Psychology and the construction of gender*. New Haven: Yale University Press.

Kimmel, M. S. (Ed.) (1987). *Changing men: New directions in research on men and masculinity*. Newbury Park, CA: Sage.

Unger, R. K., & Crawford, M. (1992). *Women and gender: A feminist psychology*. New York and Philadelphia, PA: McGraw-Hill and Temple University Press.

Wilkinson, S. A. (Ed.) (1986). *Feminist social psychology*. Milton Keynes: Open University Press.

REFERENCES

Altman, M. (1984). Everything they always wanted you to know. In C. S. Vance (Ed.) *Pleasure and danger: Exploring female sexuality* (pp. 115–130). Boston, MA: Routledge & Kegan Paul.

Apfelbaum, E. (1986). *Women in leadership positions*. Henry Tajfel Memorial Lecture presented at the annual conference of the British Psychological Society, University of Sussex.

Attie, I., & Brooks-Gunn, J. (1989). The development of eating problems in adolescent girls: A longitudinal study. *Developmental Psychology, 25,* 70–79.

Belk, S. S., Garcia-Falconi, R., Hernandez-Sanchez, J., & Snell, W. E. (1988). Avoidance strategy use in the intimate relationships of women and men from Mexico and the United States. *Psychology of Women Quarterly, 12,* 165–174.

Bell, I. P. (1989). The double standard: Age. In J. Freeman (Ed.) *Women: A feminist perspective* (4th edn, pp. 236–244). Mountain View, CA: Mayfield.

Blumstein, P., & Schwartz, P. (1983). *American couples*. New York: William Morrow.

Boston Lesbian Psychologies Collective (Eds) (1987). *Lesbian psychologies: Explorations and challenges*. Urbana, IL: University of Illinois.

Brooks-Gunn, J. (1987). The impact of puberty and sexual activity upon the health and education of adolescent girls and boys. *Peabody Journal of Education, 64,* 88–112.

Brown, L., & Root, M. (Eds) (1990). *Diversity and complexity in feminist therapy*. New York: Harrington Park Press.

Carli, L. L. (1990). Gender, language, and influence. *Journal of Personality and Social Psychology, 59,* 941–951.

Carpenter, C. J., Huston, A. C., & Holt, W. (1986). Modification of pre-school sex-typed behaviors by participation in adult-structured activities. *Sex Roles, 14,* 603–615.

Carter, D. B., & McCloskey, L. A. (1984). Peers and the maintenance of sex-typed behavior: The development of children's conceptions of cross-gender behavior in their peers. *Social Cognition, 2,* 294–314.

Chapkis, W. (1986). *Beauty secrets: Women and the politics of appearance*. Boston, MA: South End.

Charlesworth, W. R., & Dzur, C. (1987). Gender comparisons of pre-schoolers' behavior and resource utilization in group problem-solving. *Child Development, 58,* 191–200.

Chipman, S. F., & Wilson, D. M. (1985). Understanding mathematics course enrollment and mathematics achievement: A synthesis of the research. In S. F. Chipman, L. R. Brush, & D. M. Wilson (Eds) *Women and mathematics: Balancing the equation* (pp. 275–328). Hillsdale, NJ: Lawrence Erlbaum.

Crawford, M., & Marecek, J. (1989). Psychology reconstructs the female. *Psychology of Women Quarterly*, *13*, 147–166.

Crosby, F. (1982). *Relative deprivation and working women.* New York: Oxford University Press.

Crosby, F. (Ed.) (1987). *Spouse, parent, worker: On gender and multiple roles.* New Haven, CT: Yale University Press.

Deaux, K. (1985). Sex and gender. *Annual Review of Psychology*, *36*, 49–81.

Deaux, K., & Major, B. (1987). Putting gender into context: An interactive model of gender-related behavior. *Psychological Review*, *94*, 369–389.

Denmark, F., Russo, N. F., Frieze, I. H., & Sechzer, J. A. (1988). Guidelines for avoiding sexism in psychological research: A report of the ad hoc committee on nonsexist research. *American Psychologist*, *43*, 582–585.

Dion, K. L. (1985). Sex, gender, and groups. In V. E. O'Leary, R. K. Unger, & B. S. Wallston (Eds) *Women, gender, and social psychology*, Hillsdale, NJ: Lawrence Erlbaum.

Dovidio, J. F., & Gaertner, S. L. (1983). The effects of sex, status, and ability on helping behavior. *Journal of Applied Social Psychology*, *13*, 191–205.

Dovidio, J. F., Ellyson, S. L., Keating, C. F., Heltman, K., & Brown, C. E. (1988). The relationship of social power to visual displays of dominance between men and women. *Journal of Personality and Social Psychology*, *54*, 233–242.

Eagly, A. H., & Wood, W. (1982). Inferred sex differences in status as a determinant of gender stereotypes about social influence. *Journal of Personality and Social Psychology*, *43*, 915–928.

Eccles, J. S. (1989). Bringing young women to math and science. In M. Crawford & M. Gentry (Eds) *Gender and thought: Psychological perspectives* (pp. 36–58). New York: Springer-Verlag.

Eccles (Parsons), J. S., Adler, T. F., Futterman, R., Goff, S. B., Kaczala, C. M., Meece, J. L., & Midgley, C. (1985). Self-perceptions, task perceptions, socializing influences, and the decision to enroll in mathematics. In S. F. Chipman, L. R. Brush, & D. M. Wilson (Eds) *Women and mathematics: Balancing the equation* (pp. 95–122). Hillsdale, NJ: Lawrence Erlbaum.

Espin, O. M. (1986). Cultural and historical influences on sexuality in Hispanic/Latin women. In J. Cole (Ed.) *All American women: Lines that divide, ties that bind* (pp. 272–284). New York: Free Press (Macmillan).

Falbo, T., & Peplau, L. A. (1980). Power strategies in intimate relationships. *Journal of Personality and Social Psychology*, *38*, 618–628.

Fine, M. (1983–1984). Coping with rape: Critical perspectives on consciousness. *Imagination, Cognition, and Personality*, *3*, 249–267.

Fine, M. (1988). Sexuality, schooling, and adolescent females: The missing discourse of desire. *Harvard Educational Review*, *58*, 29–53.

Fine, M., & Asch, A. (1988). *Women with disabilities: Essays in psychology, culture, and politics.* Philadelphia, PA: Temple University Press.

Fine, M., & Gordon, S. M. (1989). Feminist transformations of/despite psychology. In M. Crawford and M. Gentry (Eds) *Gender and thought: Psychological Perspectives.* New York: Springer-Verlag.

Foucault, M. (1978). *The history of sexuality.* New York: Pantheon.

Freedman, R. (1986). *Beauty bound.* Lexington, MA: D. C. Heath.

Garner, D. M., Garfinkel, P. E., Schwartz, D., & Thompson, M. (1980). Cultural expectations of thinness in women. *Psychological Reports, 47*, 483–491.

Grady, K. E. (1981). Sex bias in research design. *Psychology of Women Quarterly, 5*, 628–636.

Greenspan, M. (1983). *A new approach to women and therapy.* New York: McGraw-Hill.

Hamilton, J. A., & Gallant (Alagna), S. J. (1988). On a premenstrual psychiatric diagnosis: What's in a name? *Professional Psychology: Research and Practice, 19*, 271–278.

Hare-Mustin, R. T., & Marecek, J. (Eds) (1990). *Making a difference: Psychology and the construction of gender.* New Haven, CT: Yale University Press.

Henley, N. M. (1977). *Body politics: Power, sex, and nonverbal communication.* Englewood Cliffs, NJ: Prentice-Hall.

Hesse-Biber, S. (1989). Eating patterns and disorders in a college population: Are college women's eating problems a new phenomenon? *Sex Roles, 20*, 71–89.

Hyde, J. S., & Linn, M. C. (Eds) (1986). *The psychology of gender: Advances through meta-analysis.* Baltimore, MD: Johns Hopkins University Press.

Jacklin, C. N. (1981). Methodological issues in the study of sex-related differences. *Developmental Review, 1*, 266–273.

Jackson, L. A., Sullivan, L. A., & Rostker, R. (1988). Gender, gender role, and body image. *Sex Roles, 19*, 429–443.

Jackson, M. (1987). "Facts of life" or the eroticization of women's oppression? Sexology and the social construction of heterosexuality. In P. Caplan (Ed.) *The cultural construction of sexuality* (pp. 52–81). London: Tavistock.

Kahn, A. S., & Jean, P. J. (1983). Integration and elimination or separation and redefinition: The future of the psychology of women. *Signs: Journal of Women in Culture and Society, 8*, 659–670.

Kaiser, K. (1990). Cross-cultural perspectives on menopause. In M. Flint, F. Kronenberg, & W. H. Utian (Eds) *Multidisciplinary perspectives on menopause. Annals of the New York Academy of Sciences, 592*, 430–432.

Kelley, H. H., Cunningham, J. D., Grisham, J. A., Lefebvre, L. M., Sink, C. R., & Yablon, G. (1978). Sex differences in comments made during conflict within close heterosexual pairs. *Sex Roles, 4*, 473–491.

Kimmel, D. C. (1988). Ageism, psychology, and public policy. *American Psychologist, 43*, 175–178.

Laws, J. L., & Schwartz, P. (1977). *Sexual scripts.* Hinsdale, IL: Dryden.

Leffler, A., Gillespie, D. L., & Conaty, J. C. (1982). The effects of status differentiation on nonverbal behavior. *Social Psychology Quarterly, 45*, 153–161.

Lerman, H., & Porter, N. (1990). The contribution of feminism to ethics in psychotherapy. In H. Lerman & N. Porter (Eds) *Feminist ethics in psychotherapy* (pp. 5–13). New York: Springer.

Lykes, M. B. (1989). Dialogue with Guatemalan Indian women: Critical perspectives on constructing collaborative research. In R. K. Unger (Ed.) *Representations: Social constructions of gender* (pp. 167–186). Amityville, NY: Baywood.

McCaulay, M., Mintz, L., & Glenn, A. A. (1988). Body image, self-esteem, and depression-proneness: Closing the gender gap. *Sex Roles, 18*, 381–391.

Maccoby, E. E. (1988). Gender as a social category. *Developmental Psychology, 24*, 755–765.

McGrath, E., Keita, G. P., Strickland, B. R., & Russo, N. F. (1990). *Women and depression: Risk factors and treatment issues.* Washington, DC: American Psychological Association.

McHugh, M. D., Koeske, R. D., & Frieze, I. H. (1986). Issues to consider in conducting nonsexist psychological research: A guide for researchers. *American Psychologist, 41*, 879–890.

Major, B., & Deaux, K. (1982). Individual differences in justice behavior. In J. Greenberg & R. L. Cohen (Eds) *Equity and justice in social behavior*. New York: Academic Press.

Major, B., McFarlin, D. B., & Gagnon, D. (1984). Overworked and underpaid: On the nature of gender differences in personal entitlement. *Journal of Personality and Social Psychology, 47*, 1399–1412.

Martin, E. (1987). *The woman in the body: A cultural analysis of reproduction*. Boston, MA: Beacon.

Miller, J. B. (1986). *Toward a new psychology of women*. Boston, MA: Beacon (originally published 1976).

Muehlenhard, C. L., & Linton, M. A. (1987). Date rape and sexual aggression in dating situations: Incidence and risk factors. *Journal of Counseling Psychology, 34*, 186–196.

O'Connell, A. N., & Russo, N. F. (1991). Special issue: Women's heritage in psychology: Origins, development, and future directions. *Psychology of Women Quarterly, 15*(4).

Paludi, M. A., & Strayer, L. A. (1984). What's in an author's name? Differential evaluations of performance as a function of author's name. *Sex Roles, 10*, 353–361.

Parlee, M. B. (1981). Appropriate control groups in feminist research. *Psychology of Women Quarterly, 5*, 637–644.

Peplau, L. A., & Conrad, E. (1989). Beyond nonsexist research: The perils of feminist methods in psychology. *Psychology of Women Quarterly, 13*, 379–400.

Peplau, L. A., & Gordon, S. L. (1985). Women and men in love: Gender differences in close heterosexual relationships. In V. E. O'Leary, R. K. Unger, & B. S. Wallston (Eds) *Women, gender, and social psychology* (pp. 257–292). Hillsdale, NJ: Lawrence Erlbaum.

Porter, N., & Geis, F. (1981). Women and nonverbal leadership cues: When seeing is not believing. In C. Mayo & N. Henley (Eds) *Gender and nonverbal behavior*. New York: Springer-Verlag.

Pugh, M. D., & Wahrman, R. (1983). Neutralizing sexism in mixed-sex groups: Do women have to be better than men? *American Journal of Sociology, 88*, 746–762.

Radlove, S. (1983). Sexual response and gender roles. In E. R. Allgeier & N. B. McCormick (Eds) *Changing boundaries: Gender roles and sexual behavior* (pp. 87–105). Palo Alto, CA: Mayfield.

Radway, J. (1984). *Reading the romance: Women, patriarchy, and popular literature*. Chapel Hill, NC: University of North Carolina Press.

Rhyne, D. (1981). Bases of marital satisfaction among men and women. *Journal of Marriage and the Family, 43*, 941–955.

Roopnarine, J. L. (1984). Sex-typed socialization in mixed-age preschool classrooms. *Child Development, 55*, 1078–1084.

Root, M. P. P. (1990). Disordered eating in women of color. *Sex Roles, 22*, 525–536.

Rose, S. A., & Frieze, I. H. (1989). Young singles' scripts for a first date. *Gender & Society, 3*, 258–268.

Rosenberg, R. (1982). *Beyond separate spheres: The intellectual roots of modern feminism*. New Haven, CT: Yale University Press.

Rubin, G. (1984). Thinking sex: Notes for a radical theory of the politics of sexuality. In C. S. Vance (Ed.) *Pleasure and danger: Exploring female sexuality* (pp. 267–319). Boston, MA: Routledge & Kegan Paul.

Ruble, D. N., Fleming, A. S., Hackel, L. S., & Stangor, C. (1988). Changes in the marital relationship during the transition to first time motherhood: Effects of violated expectations concerning division of household labor. *Journal of Personality and Social Psychology*, *85*, 78–87.

Russell, D. E. H. (1984). *Sexual exploitation: Rape, child sexual abuse, and workplace harassment*. Beverly Hills, CA: Sage.

Scarborough, E., & Furumoto, L. (1987). *Untold lives: The first generation of American women psychologists*. New York: Columbia University Press.

Sherif, C. W. (1982). Needed concepts in the study of gender identity. *Psychology of Women Quarterly*, *6*, 375–398.

Signorielli, N. (1989). Television and conceptions about sex roles: Maintaining conventionality and the status quo. *Sex Roles*, *21*, 341–360.

Silverstein, B., Perdue, L., Peterson, B., & Kelley, E. (1986). The role of the mass media in promoting a thin standard of bodily attractiveness for women. *Sex Roles*, *14*, 519–532.

Silverstein, B., Perdue, L., Peterson, B., Vogel, L., & Fantini, D. A. (1986). Some possible causes of the thin standard of bodily attractiveness for women. *International Journal of Eating Disorders*, *5*, 907–916.

Skrypnek, B. J., & Snyder, M. (1982). On the self-perpetuating nature of stereotypes about women and men. *Journal of Experimental Social Psychology*, *18*, 277–291.

Snyder, M., & Uranowitz, S. W. (1978). Reconstructing the past: some cognitive consequences of person perception. *Journal of Personality and Social Psychology*, *36*, 941–950.

Soley, L. C., & Kurzbard, G. (1986). Sex in advertising: A comparison of 1964 and 1984 magazine advertisements. *Journal of Advertising*, *15*, 46–64.

Stake, J., & Lauer, M. L. (1987). The consequences of being overweight: A controlled study of gender differences. *Sex Roles*, *17*, 31–37.

Steil, J. M., & Weltman, K. (1991). Marital inequality: The importance of resources, personal attributes, and social norms on career valuing and the allocation of domestic responsibilities. *Sex Roles*, *24*, 161–179.

Steinberg, L., & Silverberg, S. B. (1987). Influences on marital satisfaction during the middle stages of the family life cycle. *Journal of Marriage and the Family*, *49*, 751–760.

Stimpson, C. R. (1986). *Women's studies in the United States*. New York: Ford Foundation.

Taylor, S. E., Fiske, S. T., Etcoff, N. L., & Ruderman, A. J. (1978). Categorical and contextual bases of person memory and stereotyping. *Journal of Personality and Social Psychology*, *36*, 778–793.

Tevlin, H. E., & Leiblum, S. R. (1983). Sex-role stereotypes and female sexual dysfunction. In V. Franks & E. Rothblum (Eds) *Stereotyping of women: Its effects on mental health* (pp. 129–148). New York: Springer.

Thorne, B., & Luria, Z. (1986). Sexuality and gender in children's daily worlds. *Social Problems*, *33*, 176–190.

Towson, S. M. J., Zanna, M. P., & MacDonald, G. (1989). Self-fulfilling prophecy: Sex-role stereotypes and expectations for behavior. In R. K. Unger (Ed.) *Representations: Social constructions of gender* (pp. 97–107). Amityville, NY: Baywood.

Travis, C. (1990). *The social construction of women's sexuality*. Paper presented at the annual conference of the American Psychological Association, Boston, MA, August.

Unger, R. K. (1979). *Female and male*. New York: Harper & Row.

Unger, R. K. (1983). Through the looking glass: No Wonderland yet! (The reciprocal relationship between methodology and models of reality). *Psychology of Women Quarterly*, *8*, 9–32.

Unger, R. K. (1988). Psychological, feminist, and personal epistemology. In M. M. Gergen (Ed.) *Feminist thought and the structure of knowledge* (pp. 124–141). New York: New York University Press.

Unger, R. K. (1990). Imperfect reflections of reality. In R. I. Hare-Mustin & J. Marecek (Eds) *Making a difference: Psychology and the construction of gender* (pp. 102–149). New Haven, CT: Yale University Press.

Unger, R. K. (1992). Will the real sex difference please stand up? *Feminism & Psychology*, *2*, 231–238.

Unger, R. K., & Crawford, M. (1992). *Women and gender: A feminist psychology*. New York and Philadelphia, PA: McGraw-Hill and Temple University Press.

Ussher, J. (1989). *The psychology of the female body*. London: Routledge.

Wallston, B. S., & Grady, K. E. (1985). Integrating the feminist critique and the crisis in social psychology: Another look at research methods. In V. E. O'Leary, R. K. Unger, & B. S. Wallston (Eds) *Women, gender and social psychology* (pp. 7–34). Hillsdale, NJ: Lawrence Erlbaum.

Wallston, B. S., & O'Leary, V. E. (1981). Sex makes a difference: Differential perceptions of women and men. In L. Wheeler (Ed.) *Review of personality and social psychology* (vol. 2). Beverly Hill, CA: Sage.

West, C., & Zimmerman, D. H. (1987). Doing gender. *Gender & Society*, *1*, 125–151.

Wiley, M. G., & Eskilson, A. (1982). Coping in the corporation: Sex role constraints. *Journal of Applied Social Psychology*, *12*, 1–11.

Yarkin, K. L., Town, J. P., & Wallston, B. S. (1982). Blacks and women must try harder: Stimulus persons' race and sex and attributions of causality. *Personality and Social Psychology Bulletin*, *8*, 21–24.

4

PSYCHOLOGY AND THE LAW

Robert T. Croyle
University of Utah, USA
Elizabeth F. Loftus
University of Washington, USA

Every legal system is, in part, a way to evaluate and manage human behaviour. Hence the law makes a number of assumptions, often unstated, about human psychology. The overlap of psychology and the law has always interested psychologists. The 1908 publication of Hugo Münsterberg's *On the Witness Stand* marks the beginning of systematic psychological research on the legal system of the United States. More recently, the rise of social psychology in the 1960s led to comprehensive books and papers that rejuvenated interest in psychology and the law (Kalven & Zeisel, 1966; Tapp, 1969). Research since then has tended to focus on issues of criminal jury trials, despite the small number of such trials compared to other legal actions.

BARRIERS TO ACCEPTANCE

There are differences in the method of inquiry of the two disciplines: the law relies on doctrine and precedent, whereas psychology relies on empirical support for theory-bound hypotheses. As a result, legal judgments are clinical and diagnostic, and data from psychological research are mainly probabilistic and statistical (Doyle, 1989). Understandably, there are barriers to the law's acceptance of empirical psychology. Sometimes personal biases surface. The trial, to some psychologists, is an arena where attorneys defend preconceptions in the face of constant debate, where actual guilt or innocence is not the point. On the other hand, some lawyers believe that psychologists are inclined by temperament and training to mitigate the rigour of the law (e.g., Cederbaums & Arnold, 1975). Despite these differences, psychological studies are used more and more as evidence in trials, and as support in written court opinions (Vollrath & Davis, 1980).

Although the bulk of research deals with criminal trials, virtually every area of the legal process that touches on psychology has been investigated. It is useful to organize research by relating findings to the legal process itself. The first major phase of the judicial process involves pre-trial activities, such as influences on criminal behaviour, pre-trial publicity, and alternative methods of resolving disputes. The second phase is the trial, where research follows procedures and participants, to paraphrase the classification suggested by Thibaut and Walker (1975). Trial procedures involve the organization of the trial and competence to stand trial. Participants include information suppliers such as witnesses, and judges and juries as decision-makers. Finally, research on sentencing and incarceration includes sentencing disparity and prison confinement.

PRE-TRIAL

Pre-trial publicity

Often the media report details of a crime before it comes to trial; potential jurors may have knowledge and opinions about a case before hearing any evidence in trial. The prejudicial impact of pre-trial publicity operates in a number of specific ways. Some researchers distinguish between factual publicity, which might include incriminating evidence, and emotional publicity, which usually takes the form of a dramatic appeal to the emotions. For both of these types of publicity, the more that witnesses have been exposed to such information, the more they will tend to favour the prosecution in trial. Judges' instructions have no appreciable effect on biases from pre-trial publicity, and deliberation usually strengthens these publicity biases. Although most jurors who have been exposed to "anti-defence" publicity do not report any partiality, they perceive the defendant as being more guilty than do jurors who have not been exposed (Kramer, Kerr, & Carroll, 1990). Even gossip may have a role in prejudicial publicity: testimony following discussion of the facts of a case includes false information at a much greater rate than testimony with no prior discussion. This result did not, however, hold for narrative recall of simple information (Hollin & Clifford, 1983).

Alternatives to a formal trial

Alternatives to trial decisions arose primarily during the 1970s in the United States as a method of reducing backlog and delay in the court system. One method was the Summary Jury Trial, which utilized a videotape of trial proceedings, edited for clarity by the judge. The resulting jury verdict took on the character of advice to the court rather than a binding decision such as a jury verdict. Experimental confirmation of the utility of the Summary Jury Trial is mixed and sparse.

TRIAL

Procedures

Research related specifically to the process of the trial involves issues with the trial's procedures or participants. This distinction is pragmatic only, and not clear-cut in every instance.

Research indicates that European and American subjects tend to think of their native judicial system as more fair, regardless of whether their countries employ an adversary or non-adversary system. The adversary system somewhat reduces expectancy biases, but increases the chance that pertinent information will not reach the trier of fact (Walker & Lind, 1984). Other procedural research suggests that the chronological order in which jurors receive information affects their judgement about defendants. For example, if attorneys present charges against a defendant in reverse order of severity, then juries are more inclined to find against the defendant. These relationships hold both for mock juries (groups who deliberate about a decision) and for mock jurors (individuals) (Davis, 1989). Multiple charges against a defendant in a single trial may increase the rate of guilty verdicts, over the rate found with independent consideration of the charges. In addition, experienced jurors may be more likely than uninitiated jurors to convict a suspect (Davis, Tindale, Nagao, Hinsz, & Robertson, 1984).

Participants: information suppliers

Eyewitness testimony

Eyewitness testimony is a highly popular area of psychology and law research. Generally, memory for the events of a crime involves the same issues as does memory for any other event. The process of memory roughly comprises the acquisition, retention, and retrieval stages. For memory acquisition, some factors relate directly to the criminal act. For example, witnesses tend drastically to overestimate crime duration, a phenomenon typical of memory for complex or rapid events. Victims also tend to remember fewer details, especially peripheral details, as the violence of the crime increases. Other research on event factors covers lighting conditions, speed, distance, and colour vision (Loftus, Greene, & Doyle, 1989).

Characteristics of the witness have also been related to memory acquisition. For instance, most studies conclude that memory for everyday facts does not improve with a witness's training or experience. Although women are better than men at recognizing faces in some laboratory studies, this does not seem to be the case in the eyewitness context (Loftus, Banaji, Schooler, & Foster, 1987). Finally, when witnesses have different preconceptions or prior expectations relating to some element of a crime, their recall of events may vary widely.

The role of age in an eyewitness's accuracy has also been examined. Adult memory performance declines with advancing age, on the average. Children often recall less than adults, although they can be quite accurate in what they do recall. Children tend to make more errors when responding to specific questions, and young children tend to be more suggestible than adults (Doris, 1991).

Stress and arousal during a crime can influence recall in a number of ways. The Yerkes-Dodson Law states that performance is best at a certain optimum level of stress, and that an increase or decrease in stress from this level will accompany a decline in performance (Yerkes & Dodson, 1908). Tolerance for stress varies from person to person. Experimental research findings tend to agree with this model, although one field study found that reported stress did not impair accurate memory (Yuille & Cutshall, 1986). The relation between stress and accurate memory is hard to evaluate, but it seems clear that stress restricts attention. In particular, witnesses to crimes with weapons often experience "weapon focus" – concentration on a visible weapon to the exclusion of other details of the situation. Chronic stress on a person, such as is brought on by the loss of a job or death in the family, can also reduce memory (Loftus, Greene, & Doyle, 1989).

Memory retention is influenced by time and by post-event information. Ebbinghaus's forgetting curve suggests that memory declines rapidly soon after an event, and then declines gradually. Many studies support this trend for eyewitness memory (e.g., Cash & Moss, 1972). Beyond the effect of time, the stress of a violent or emotional event may motivate a witness to "forget" an unpleasant incident. Memory is also malleable and subject to distortions. Information that may not be true about a crime reaches witnesses through

61

Figure 1 Materials used in memory experiment. These photographs were used in an experiment designed to test the accuracy of recollection of two groups of subjects. The only difference between the two photos is that there is a stop sign in one and a yield (give way) sign in the other
Source: Loftus, Miller, and Burns, 1978

conversation, newspapers, and television, and even through questions about the crime posed to them by the authorities.

Additional information, true or false, can supplement or distort true memories. Loftus, Miller, and Burns (1978) showed subjects a series of colour slides depicting an accident. A red car was shown approaching an intersection. After turning a corner, the car knocked down a pedestrian who was crossing the street. One of the slides was varied (see Figure 1). Half of the subjects saw the slide with the stop sign, whereas others saw the slide with the yield (give way) sign. Immediately afterward, some subjects were asked a series of questions that included, "Did another car pass the red Datsun while it was stopped at the stop sign?" On a later memory test, subjects who answered this question after seeing the slide with a yield sign were more likely to remember seeing a stop sign. These effects of false information grow as the original memory fades in time. Warning a witness about the possibility of misleading information reduces the chance of memory distortion.

Legal procedures require witnesses to retrieve all kinds of information from memory. Witnesses might identify particular objects or people, or simply give general impressions. As the Loftus et al. (1978) study described above illustrates, the method of eliciting information plays a large role in accuracy. The most fruitful interview strategy is for the witness first to report freely about the crime and then to answer specific questions. Even small differences in question wording can produce different answers. For example, researchers found that asking, "Did you see the broken headlight?" led to more wrong affirmations than did the question, "Did you see a broken headlight?" The greater the perceived credibility of the questioner, the more easily witnesses can be misled. Laws of procedure are intended to prevent the courtroom use of many types of leading questions. Nevertheless, many interviews take place before the witness is in court. The importance of unbiased interviews and identification procedures prior to trial cannot be overstated (Wells, 1993).

Jurors are often impressed with witnesses who are conspicuously confident or detailed about their own testimonies. Unfortunately, most research findings conclude that the relationship between confidence and accuracy in testimony is not a strong one. When a single witness is partly confident and partly hesitant in testimony, the confidently stated information is slightly more likely to be correct (Loftus et al., 1989). The relation of confidence to accuracy is positively strengthened when witnesses watch videotapes of themselves making an identification, and then rate their confidence in their identifications (Kassin, 1985).

Assessing and improving the validity of testimony

Social scientists and legal professionals have developed several interview methods with a view to maximizing recall accuracy. Most research has been devoted to the hypnosis, cognitive, and polygraph interview methods. The phenomenon of hypnosis is complex and not thoroughly understood (Sigman, Philips, & Clifford, 1985). Dramatic cases exist where hypnosis interviews appeared to enhance recall for otherwise inaccessible information, but the method is not considered reliable by many court jurisdictions in the USA. Common misunderstandings about the nature of hypnosis and conflicting research results hinder its acceptance. For instance, popular films often depict hypnotists as able to control their hypnotized subjects' minds. No research finding supports this belief. Another misunderstanding is that hypnotized subjects *ipso facto* tell the truth; actually there is no medical or psychological method known to ensure truthfulness. Hypersuggestibility is sometimes attributed to subjects in a hypnosis interview (Reiser, 1989). Other commentators maintain that hypnosis interviews increase in reported testimony the amount of confabulation, or the filling in of memory gaps with invented information, in testimony. In addition, hypnotized witnesses can later become overconfident of their memories (Wrightsman, 1991).

The close similarity between part of the hypnosis interview and the cognitive interview format prompted some researchers to investigate the comparative utility of the two methods. The cognitive interview was developed to help standardize and improve the interviewing skills of law enforcers. Cognitive interviews use the same general format as a "standard" interview: free recall followed by specific questions, but it also contains certain general memory enhancement features. The close similarity of the preparation steps for the hypnosis interview and the cognitive interview itself may be responsible for a large part of improved memory under hypnosis, rather than the hypnotic state itself (Yuille & Kim, 1987). At the beginning of an interview, a witness receives instructions on these techniques. For example, a common version of the cognitive interview includes instructions to reinstate the crime's context, be complete, recall information in varying sequences, and change perspectives. Mentally reconstructing the crime's context helps to make recall more complete, and may be better than actually revisiting the crime scene since the scene may have changed. Such context reinstatement is a particular aid in accurate memory for facial details (Davies & Milne, 1985). Enjoining witnesses to be complete keeps them from withholding information that they think is not important, and may increase mental associations. Changing perspectives involves thinking about the incident from different points of view, and may help recall for details. Generally, cognitive interviews produce more correct information than standard interviews, and with no accompanying increase in incorrect recall. There is some evidence that cognitive interviews may help reduce the effects of leading questions relative to a standard interview. The cognitive interview can be applied to adults and children (Geiselman & Fisher, 1989).

Perhaps the most notorious forensic interview method is the polygraph interview (the "lie-detector test"). Polygraphy had an inauspicious start in the time of Münsterberg, and evolved to measuring blood pressure and respiratory changes in the 1930s. In the 1990s polygraph devices measure these two variables and electrodermal response, perspiration, and peripheral vascular activity. Polygraph relies on physiological responses to psychological changes. The fact that such responses exist seems obvious – blushing, nervous perspiration, and so on – but many emotions such as anger, excitement, fear, or guilt produce similar physiological responses. The problem for polygraph is to tease out the effects of particular emotions while controlling for the effects of any others. The ability of polygraph to isolate and distinguish these effects is a matter of wide debate (Wrightsman, 1991).

There are two types of polygraph techniques. The first type is the deception test, where a person is overtly tested for deceit. The second is the information test, where a person is tested for knowledge of or involvement in a particular crime. Questions on deception tests must refer only to information for which a person has clear memory, and must be phrased in such a way that the person can answer only yes or no. Questions should not ask for interpretations or conclusions. One type of deception test is the relevant-irrelevant test, which is composed of neutral questions such as, "Is today March 15th?" and relevant questions such as, "Did you take the diamonds from the jewellery case?" The basis for scoring the test is the assumption that guilty people will conceal their involvement in a crime, and will answer "no" to relevant questions. Although they answer no, the polygraph will detect an involuntary autonomic response that the polygrapher can compare to the neutral question responses. Validity for relevant-irrelevant questions is low for two reasons: innocent subjects can be very anxious when presented relevant questions, and people with unusual reactivity in general confuse the test (Raskin, 1989).

A second type of deception test is the control question test. The control question test compares reactions to relevant questions with reactions to control questions. Control questions ask about acts that most people have engaged in but are motivated to conceal during a proper polygraph interview. For example, a control question might be, "In the first 25 years of your life, did you ever take something that did not belong to you?" The polygrapher reviews these questions with the subject before the actual polygraph interview in such a way that the subject will answer them in the negative (even when this is not true). The basis for scoring the control question test is the assumption that innocent subjects will produce noticeably stronger reactions to control questions than to relevant questions, and that the opposite will hold for guilty subjects (Kircher & Raskin, 1992).

Experimental tests of polygraph validity have the advantage of knowing whether a subject was truthful or deceptive, while field studies must infer this information from confessions. In experimental studies, rates of correct classification for guilty and innocent subjects range from 50 per cent to nearly 100 per cent. A reason for these divergent findings may be the difficulty of recreating the strong emotional atmosphere of a real polygraph interview (Wrightsman, 1991). Field studies show consistently higher rates of correct classification. Even computerized scoring methods have been introduced to polygraph. Regardless of these findings, polygraph evidence is admitted in court either with strong stipulations, or not at all (Kircher & Raskin, 1992).

Information tests assess not deception, but the likelihood of a subject's knowledge of certain information. The most frequently used information test is the concealed knowledge test, originally referred to as the guilty knowledge test. This format requires the polygrapher to have information about a crime that is not known to the public. The subject's electrodermal responses to multiple-choice questions such as, "Regarding the weapon used to stab the victim, do you know if it was: (a) a bread knife, (b) an icepick, or (c) a screw-driver?" The assumption underlying this approach is that the electrodermal response will be strongest in response to the correct item for individuals with knowledge about the crime. Experimental research on concealed knowledge tests is encouraging, but there are no published attempts to replicate these findings in field settings (Raskin, 1989).

Opponents of polygraphy and deception tests cite the enormous complexity of human physiological responses. The ostensible accuracy rate of the poly-graph is an artifact, they argue, stemming from the individual's likelihood of confessing in the face of a "deceptive" polygraph result, regardless of whether the person is actually responsible for the crime. An argument against the use of control question polygraphy is that the method relies on certain interpersonal abilities of the polygrapher, such as the polygrapher's ability to consistently deceive the person taking the examination. Research on the validity of polygraphy is difficult to interpret for a number of reasons. First, experimental settings with volunteer subjects may not recreate the same level of emotional arousal found in someone accused of a crime. Second, studies involving real defendants often cannot be validated by subsequent confessions, for reasons just mentioned (Lykken, 1992).

Besides witnesses, videotapes of crime scenes have been studied as in-formation suppliers to the courtroom process. Findings of mock jury studies suggest that videotapes of crime scenes can prejudice criminal trials. In one study, mock jurors viewed videotapes of a murder victim and the scene of the crime. Other mock jurors saw a videotape from an unrelated case, and a third group saw no videotape at all. Two days later at a mock trial, jurors who saw the first videotape set lower standards of evidentiary proof and showed stronger juror biases than did jurors from the other two groups (e.g., Kassin & Garfield, 1991).

Psychologists as expert witnesses

Psychologists participate in trials in two ways. First, clinical psychologists may offer testimony regarding some set of symptoms displayed by a particu-lar victim or defendant. Such testimony can take the form of a competency evaluation based on diagnostic tests. A second sort of testimony offered by psychologists is "social framework" testimony, where a psychologist presents statistical analyses and findings of relevant scientific research. Testimony of this latter type is often restricted to broad topics such as the psychological effects of discrimination in the workplace (Loftus, 1991).

When presenting this second sort of testimony, psychologists are acting as "expert witnesses". In 1975 the United States Congress codified the Federal Rules of Evidence. Rule 702 requires that expert witnesses "assist the trier of fact to understand the evidence or to determine a fact in issue". The *Frye* decision of 1923 set criteria for admissibility of expert testimony that augment the Federal Rules of Evidence. Experts must confine their testimony to theory that is generally accepted by psychologists, and their testimony must be such that its probative value is not outweighed by its prejudicial value in the eyes of the court. Judges interpret the wording of these guidelines of admissibility on a case-by-case basis (Goodman & Loftus, 1992).

Clearly expert psychological testimony can bear on matters crucial to the disposition of a case, such as the accuracy of eyewitness testimony. The law has, in effect, a series of screens designed to eliminate unreliable evidence. In addition to the Federal Rules of Evidence and the *Frye* criteria, judges can admit or reject evidence based on various legal idiosyncrasies that a particular case might pose. The role of the expert psychological witness is to be part of this screen for evidence, especially on the issues of perception, memory, and extenuating circumstances. The use of psychologists as expert witnesses appears to be increasing, and accompanying this increase is legal and psychological debate about the efficacy of their testimony.

Many legal arguments against psychological experts relate to the possible reaction of juries. A common warning is that juries may be overpersuaded by a testifying psychologist and assume that the expert testimony is infallible. In fact, experimental evidence suggests that expert testimony may cause juries to deliberate longer. One study reported that expert testimony accounts for only 3 per cent of the variance in jury verdicts (Hosch, Beck, & McIntyre, 1980). In addition, people tend to favour clinical, specific, and personal details of a situation over statistical data when making decisions, even if they are told beforehand that decisions based on statistical information have been preferable in the past. Psychological experts are also subjected to rigorous cross-examination in trials; their testimony does not pass unchallenged (Doyle, 1989).

A second variety of legal argument against experts is that the information in their testimony can be conveyed to the court without them. For example, an expert might testify that eyewitness confidence has a very small correlation with eyewitness accuracy. An attorney instead might introduce research summaries as part of a proposed instruction to the jury. Opponents of this objection claim that judges and lawyers cannot be familiar with *all* the relevant research. Some Supreme Court decisions have drawn conclusions about witness behaviour that stand in opposition to established psychological findings

(Goodman & Loftus, 1992). Even where written court opinions have made reference to psychological studies, these studies are sometimes misinterpreted (Davis, 1989).

A third legal argument against psychological experts is that jurors will misinterpret the role of the expert in court. The jury may expect testimony to be specific to the parties in trial. Jury members may therefore wrongly think that framework testimony about, say, the general unreliability of time estimates from eyewitnesses directly refutes the estimate of a particular eyewitness whose testimony is germane to the case's disposition. Federal Rule of Evidence 704 allows expert opinion testimony on the particular "ultimate issue" to be decided in a case, but such testimony might not conform to the parameters of accepted methods of scientific inference.

Opposition to social framework testimony from psychologists rests on a belief in the incompatibility of empirical psychology and formal jurisprudence. The reason for this incompatibility may be that scientific findings cannot apply to issues in single cases with particular defendants, from either ungeneralizable experimental methods or conflicting results in similar studies. A second reason is that the adversary legal system may be by nature unsuited to the rigorous and candid pursuit of facts. For example, the forgetting curve of memory has a certain shape: memory falls off rapidly after an event and then levels off. Yet the rate at which memory drops is different for different people, and different for various memories within an individual. Therefore, the argument runs, confidence in expert witness testimony on this subject is unwarranted.

There are several options in conveying psychological findings to courts. Besides expert witnesses, there are *amicus curiae* (friend of the court) briefs written by psychologists for judges. Such briefs allow summaries of psychological data. Some psychologists argue that research findings should not be treated as testimony, but as legal precedent (e.g., Monahan & Walker, 1988). Another option is to write instructions for the jury regarding relevant studies. Drawbacks of these options are that instructions may be hard to interpret or weigh properly, and that with such written information there is no opportunity for cross-examination (Goodman & Loftus, 1992).

As the debate has continued, courts have broadened the acceptability of expert testimony by psychologists in both criminal and civil cases. Courts are increasingly willing to admit expert testimony that does not purport to refer directly to parties involved in the case at hand (framework testimony); for example, psychologists have provided testimony that describes both general research findings as well as their application to the specific case at hand (Colman, 1991; Fiske, Bersoff, Borgida, Deaux, & Heilman, 1991; Goodman & Croyle, 1989). The United States Supreme Court, for example, accepted the testimony of a social psychologist in an important sex discrimination case (Fiske et al., 1991). In that case, the expert provided testimony concerning research on stereotyping, as well as opinions regarding the role of stereotyping in the evaluation of a woman under consideration for promotion.

Participants: decision-makers

Relatively few trials, civil or criminal, require juries. None the less, a large body of research exists on jury decision-making. Jury members, ideally, must weigh evidence without prejudice and reach a legal decision about human actions. Many times a jury makes decisions of importance to the community. Psychological research aims to evaluate just how well the jury performs its role. Jury decisions have been shown to relate to characteristics of the jurors themselves, and also to constraints of the legal system.

The law assumes that jurors can put aside personal biases when in court. Yet despite screening methods devised to eliminate prejudiced jurors, often jurors show bias during trial deliberations. Research into demographic characteristics of jurors has been inconclusive. Race, gender, age, religion, and education do not appear to be strongly linked with verdicts. Not even combinations of these factors can produce particularly reliable information about jury decisions. Research into juror personality characteristics shows some predictive power. First, research into locus of control shows that jurors with internal locus of control form negative attitudes more readily against defendants than do externals. Yet, locus of control seems to be unrelated to verdicts. Similarly, belief in a just world, as defined by Lerner (1980), predicts attitudes towards trial material but not legal decisions. The context of the trial, the mass of information and legal constraints, appear to outweigh these personal characteristics.

Somewhat stronger relationships hold in studies of "authoritarianism". Authoritarians are characterized by a rigid adherence to traditional middle-class values and a submissive attitude toward authority figures. High scorers on scales measuring authoritarianism are more likely to vote guilty both before and after group deliberation. Yet there are important contextual factors. For example, a juror with an authoritarian personality is less punitive towards police officers or dutiful military personnel. Thus personality characteristics do not operate without reference to the information of the particular case in question (Gerbasi, Zuckerman, & Reis, 1977). Another attitude that is relevant concerns the amount of money available for compensation. Some studies have found that plaintiffs are generally awarded more money if injured by a corporation than an individual. In addition, awards for plaintiffs are larger for defendants who are covered by insurance.

Jurors must assess the credibility of other participants and information providers in a trial (e.g. Williams, Bourgeois, Croyle, in press). Non-evidentiary factors such as facial expressions play a large role in evaluations of credibility. Even in the methodical atmosphere of the courtroom, such factors are essentially "commonsensical" and are moderately accurate at best.

Research suggests that jurors focus their attention automatically on the facial expressions of witnesses, apparently looking for cues to the unconscious content of a verbal message. Unfortunately, since people pay most attention to their facial expressions when under scrutiny, the face is fairly uninformative about truth or deception. Body, hand, and foot movement can be more reliable indicators, as can be tone of voice and hesitations in speech. These findings suggest that if a witness cannot be present to offer testimony during a trial, a videotaped deposition is superior to a message read by a court official.

Factors such as the attractiveness of the defendant play a role in jury verdicts. For example, jurors are more likely to find an unattractive defendant guilty when the victim is attractive than vice versa, even when the facts of the cases are identical. Even small changes in facial features to make an unconscious appeal to impressions of honesty, such as large eyes and high eyebrows, can affect the jury's verdict (Berry & Zebrowitz-McArthur, 1988).

Juries display common patterns of group interaction during deliberation. Although the ideal is for each juror to participate equally without domination of other jury members, in reality some jurors emerge as leaders of their group's opinions. Factors relating to opinion leadership include gender, employment and socio-economic status, and prior jury experience. Most jury leaders are male, hold jobs with more prestige than their fellows, and those with jury experience are selected as forepersons at a higher-than-normal rate. Even such arbitrary factors as seating position exert a strong influence on group leadership: jurors seated at the head of a rectangular table tend to dominate discussion during deliberation.

The deliberation process generally produces a more lenient attitude toward defendants on the part of the jury (MacCoun & Kerr, 1988). Since the majority opinion usually prevails, the collective opinions of the jurors before deliberation generally predict the verdict. In addition, some studies show that the verdict is predictable from the jurors' mid-trial opinions. Fortunately, jurors seem more receptive to new relevant information than to pressure to conform.

The legal system also strongly influences jury behaviour – overtly and covertly. Three areas of research into systemic factors in jury verdicts are the process of juror selection, the inclusion of non-evidence in the trial proceedings, and judges' instructions to juries. When selecting jurors, trial lawyers employ a variety of intuitive criteria that may have nothing to do with the legally sanctioned disposition of a case, such as the emotional impact of facial features or favouritism towards certain sports teams. Findings on the effectiveness of these methods are mixed, and there is considerable variation in the accuracy of different lawyers when screening potential jurors. Scientific jury selection, to be effective, must focus very narrowly on the specific facts of the case at hand. Demographic information of this sort is so specific that often no helpful research exists.

During the trial juries are exposed to information that is not admissible as evidence, information that none the less can affect verdicts. For example, lawyers' opening and closing statements can include recapitulations of evidence, interpretations of evidence, and alternative explanations of the crime. Jurors must be able to weed out the relevant evidence from the possibly self-interested formulations of lawyers, since the legal system permits such non-evidence in trial. A special case of non-evidence exists in testimony that is ruled inadmissible by the judge. Research shows that forbidding a jury to use some bit of evidence can have exactly the opposite effect (Wolf & Montgomery, 1977). The reason for this paradoxical effect seems not to be because of deceit or rebelliousness, but rather because jurors find such information much more salient after instructions to disregard it.

Judges sometimes give other instructions to juries, regarding the application of points of law to the evidence of the case at hand. The timing of these instructions relative to presentation of evidence is crucial. When juries received instructions before hearing evidence, the instructions had a beneficial impact on their ability to integrate facts and law (Smith, 1991). There seems to be very little difference in verdicts between juries that had no instructions and juries that received instructions after the evidence was presented. Juries provided with written or videotaped instructions from the judge seem to benefit from a clarification of the issues in a case (Kassin & Wrightsman, 1988).

SENTENCING AND INCARCERATION

Juries

Jurors weigh a large number of factors when choosing sentences for convicted defendants. Nevertheless, three factors have emerged from research as predictors of sentence severity. The first factor, prior experience on a jury, has long been suspected by attorneys as having an impact on sentencing. In an archival study of 143 criminal trials resulting in convictions, Himelein, Nietzel, and Dillehay (1991) found that more experienced juries gave significantly more severe sentences than did the less experienced juries. Whether the prior experience was on a criminal or civil case did not matter.

Wrightsman (1991) has summarized evidence indicating that women receive less severe sentences than men. When cases are matched on a number of factors, however, this difference diminishes. The same author notes evidence that American offenders convicted of murdering whites are more likely to receive the death penalty than those convicted of murdering blacks.

Judges

Like juries, judges can vary in their interpretation of the law. Sometimes disagreements among judges are quite wide, and include differences on the question of whether a criminal should be incarcerated at all. Sentences vary from state to state, court to court, and judge to judge. Studies into alternative methods of trial management and disposition, for instance review panels, also show considerable disparity. In accounting for different sentences imposed by different judges, the factor that accounts for most of the variability is the different value of legal objectives held by each judge. Less important but still prominent factors comprise the facts of the case and the political party of the judge. Special methodological problems exist in studying sources of sentencing variability. Years of special legal experience cannot be duplicated in a controlled experimental setting by lay subjects. In addition, studies involving appellate decisions are seriously confounded by different evidence and circumstances between the original and appellate trials (Palys & Divorski, 1986).

Prison confinement

There are both psychological and physiological effects to confinement in prison. Although there is no evidence for changes in cognitive functioning while in prison, inmates report being unable clearly to visualize the future beyond their prison sentences. Crowding in prisons is associated with increases in suicides, disciplinary infractions, and commitments to psychiatric wards. There are also personal factors that influence an inmate's adjustment to prison. For example, inmates who come from large families have an easier time adjusting to prison life. Other characteristics that help adjustment include previous prison experience and upbringing in an urban area. Higher educational attainment, higher socio-economic status, and being in a minority relative to the prison population are all characteristics that relate to negative reactions to prison and poorer adjustment to prison life (Paulus, 1988).

The study of physiological effects of prison confinement is complex. On the face of it, prisoners seem to have more medical problems than comparable populations outside. Prisoners have a higher-than-normal incidence of alcoholism and drug addiction on entry into prison. In addition, medical care is more readily available to prisoners than to a large percentage of the non-incarcerated population (e.g., Paulus & Dzindolet, 1992).

CONCLUSION

Given the short history of empirical research on psychological aspects of legal systems, the significant progress of this subfield is impressive. As the body of research continues to grow, so will the pressures to reform the system in a manner consistent with social scientific knowledge. Many of the goals of modern legal systems and scientific psychology are compatible, and psychologists are well equipped to assist in the development of methods to further the fair and effective application of the law. What remains to be seen, however, is whether the contributions of psychology to criminal law and procedure will be complemented by equally substantial contributions to civil law.

FURTHER READING

Davis, J. H. (1989). Psychology and law: The last 15 years. *Journal of Applied Social Psychology*, *19*, 199–230.

Raskin, D. C. (Ed.) (1989). *Psychological methods in criminal investigation and evidence*. New York: Springer.

Kassin, S. M., & Wrightsman, L. S. (1988). *The American jury on trial: Psychological perspectives*. New York: Hemisphere.

Wrightsman, L. S. (1991). *Psychology and the legal system*. Belmont, CA: Wadsworth.

REFERENCES

Berry, D. S., & Zebrowitz-McArthur, L. (1988). What's in a face: Facial maturity and the attribution of legal responsibility. *Personality and Social Psychology Bulletin*, *14*, 23–33.

Cash, W. S., & Moss, A. J. (1972). Optimum recall period for reporting persons injured in motor vehicle accidents (*DHEW – HSM Publication no. 72-1050*). Washington, DC: US Government Printing Office.

Cederbaums, J., & Arnold, S. (1975). *Scientific and expert evidence in criminal advocacy*. New York: Practicing Law Institute.

Coleman, A. M. (1991). Crowd psychology in South African murder trials. *American Psychologist*, *46*, 1071–1079.

Davies, G., & Milne, A. (1985). Eyewitness composite production: A function of mental or physical reinstatement of context. *Criminal Justice and Behavior 12*, 209–220.

Davis, J. H. (1989). Psychology and law: The last 15 years. *Journal of Applied Social Psychology*, *19*, 199–230.

Davis, J. H., Tindale, R. S., Nagao, D. H., Hinsz, V. B., & Robertson, B. (1984). Order effects in multiple decisions by group: A demonstration with mock juries and trial procedures. *Journal of Personality and Social Psychology*, *47*, 1003–1012.

Doris, J. (Ed.) (1991). *The suggestibility of children's recollections: Implications for eyewitness testimony*. Washington, DC: American Psychological Association.

Doyle, J. M. (1989). Legal issues in eyewitness evidence. In D. C. Raskin (Ed.) *Psychological methods in criminal investigation and evidence* (pp. 125–147). New York: Springer.

Fiske, S. T., Bersoff, D. N., Borgida, E., Deaux, K., & Heilman, M. E. (1991). Social science research on trial: Use of sex stereotyping research in *Price Waterhouse v. Hopkins*. *American Psychologist*, *46*, 1049–1060.

Geiselman, R. E., & Fisher, R. P. (1989). The cognitive interview technique for victims and witnesses of crime. In D. C. Raskin (Ed.) *Psychological methods in criminal investigation and evidence* (pp. 191–215). New York: Springer.

Gerbasi, K. C., Zuckerman, M., & Reis, H. T. (1977). Justice needs a new blindfold: A review of mock jury research. *Psychological Bulletin*, *84*, 323–345.

Goodman, J., & Croyle, R. T. (1989). Social framework testimony in employment discrimination cases. *Behavioral Sciences and the Law*, 7, 227–241.

Goodman, J., & Loftus, E. F. (1992). Judgement and memory: The role of expert psychological testimony on eyewitness accuracy. In P. Suedfeld & P. Tetlock (Eds) *Psychology and social policy* (pp. 267–282). New York: Hemisphere.

Himelein, M. J., Nietzel, M. T., & Dillehay, R. C. (1991). Effects of prior juror experience on jury sentencing. *Behavioral Sciences and the Law*, 9, 97–106.

Hollin, C. R., & Clifford, B. R. (1983). Eyewitness testimony: The effects of discussion on recall accuracy and agreement. *Journal of Applied Social Psychology*, 13, 234–244.

Hosch, H. M., Beck, E. L., & McIntyre, P. (1980). Influence of expert testimony regarding eyewitness accuracy on jury decisions. *Law and Human Behavior*, 4, 287–296.

Kalven, H., & Zeisel, H. (1966). *The American jury*. Boston, MA: Little, Brown.

Kassin, S. M. (1985). Eyewitness identification: Retrospective self-awareness and the accuracy-confidence correlation. *Journal of Personality and Social Psychology*, 49, 878–893.

Kassin, S. M., & Garfield, D. A. (1991). Blood and guts: General and trial-specific effects of videotaped crime scenes on mock jurors. *Journal of Applied Social Psychology*, 21, 1459–1472.

Kassin, S. M., & Wrightsman, L. S. (1988). *The American jury on trial: Psychological perspectives*. New York: Hemisphere.

Kircher, J. C., & Raskin, D. C. (1992). Polygraph techniques: History, controversies, and prospects. In P. Suedfeld & P. Tetlock (Eds) *Psychology and social policy* (pp. 295–308). New York: Hemisphere.

Kramer, G. P., Kerr, N. L., & Carroll, J. S. (1990). Pretrial publicity, judicial remedies, and jury bias. Special issue: Law and the media. *Law and Human Behavior*, 14, 409–438.

Lerner, M. J. (1980). *The belief in a just world: A fundamental delusion*. New York: Plenum.

Loftus, E. F. (1991). Resolving legal questions with psychological data. *American Psychologist*, 46, 1046–1048.

Loftus, E. F., Greene. E. L., & Doyle, J. M. (1989). The psychology of expert testimony. In D. C. Raskin (Ed.) *Psychological methods in criminal investigation and evidence* (pp. 3–45). New York: Springer.

Loftus, E. F., Miller, D. G., & Burns, H. J. (1978). Semantic integration of verbal information into a visual memory. *Journal of Experimental Psychology: Human Learning and Memory*, 4, 19–31.

Loftus, E. F., Banaji, M. R., Schooler, J. W., & Foster, R. A. (1987). Who remembers what? Gender differences in memory. *Michigan Quarterly Review*, 26, 64–85.

Lykken, D. T. (1992). Controversy: The fight-or-flight response in *Homo scientificus*. In P. Suedfeld & P. Tetlock (Eds) *Psychology and social policy* (pp. 309–325). New York: Hemisphere.

MacCoun, R. J., & Kerr, N. L. (1988). Asymmetric influence in mock jury deliberation: Jurors' bias for leniency. *Journal of Personality and Social Psychology*, 54, 21–33.

Monahan, J., & Walker, L. (1988). Social science research in law. *American Psychologist*, 43, 465–472.

Münsterberg, H. (1908). *On the witness stand*. New York: Little, Brown.

Palys, T. S., & Divorski, S. (1986). Explaining sentence disparity. *Canadian Journal of Criminology*, 28, 347–362.

Paulus, P. B. (1988). *Prison crowding: A psychological perspective*. New York: Springer-Verlag.

Paulus, P. B., & Dzindolet, M. T. (1992). The effects of prison confinement. In P. Suedfeld & P. Tetlock (Eds) *Psychology and social policy* (pp. 327–354). New York: Hemisphere.

Raskin, D. C. (1989). Polygraph techniques for the detection of deception. In D. C. Raskin (Ed.) *Psychological methods in criminal investigation and evidence* (pp. 247–296). New York: Springer.

Reiser, M. (1989). Investigative hypnosis. In D. C. Raskin (Ed.) *Psychological methods in criminal investigation and evidence* (pp. 151–190). New York: Springer.

Sigman, A., Philips, K. C., & Clifford, B. R. (1985). Attentional concomitants of hypnotic susceptibility. *British Journal of Experimental and Clinical Hypnosis, 2,* 69–75.

Smith, V. L. (1991). Impact of pretrial instruction on jurors' information processing and decision making. *Journal of Applied Psychology, 76,* 220–228.

Tapp, J. L. (1969). Psychology and the law: The dilemma. *Psychology Today, 2,* 16–22.

Thibaut, J., & Walker, L. (1975). *Procedural justice: A psychological analysis*. Hillsdale, NJ: Lawrence Erlbaum.

Vollrath, D. A., & Davis, J. H. (1980). Jury size and decision rule. In R. J. Simon, (Ed.) *The jury: Its role in American society*. Lexington, MA: Lexington Books.

Walker, L., & Lind, E. A. (1984). Psychological studies of procedural models. In G. M. Stephenson & J. H. Davis (Eds) *Progress in applied social psychology* (vol. 2). Chichester: Wiley.

Wells, G. L. (1993). What do we know about eyewitness identification? *American Psychologist, 48,* 553–571.

Williams, K. D., Bourgeois, M. J., & Croyle, R. T. (in press). The effects of stealing thunder in criminal and civil trials. *Law and Human Behavior*.

Wolf, S., & Montgomery, D. A. (1977). Effects of inadmissible evidence and level of judicial admonishment to disregard on the judgments of mock jurors. *Journal of Applied Social Psychology, 7,* 205–219.

Wrightsman, L. S. (1991). *Psychology and the legal system*. Belmont, CA: Wadsworth.

Yerkes, R. M., & Dodson, J. D. (1908). The relation of strength of stimulus to rapdity of habit-formation. *Journal of Comparative Neurology and Psychology, 18,* 459–482.

Yuille, J. C., & Cutshall, J. L. (1986). A case study of eyewitness memory of a crime. *Journal of Applied Psychology, 71,* 291–301.

Yuille, J. C., & Kim, C. K. (1987). A field study of the forensic use of hypnosis. *Canadian Journal of Behavioural Science, 19,* 418–429.

5

HEALTH PSYCHOLOGY

John Weinman
Guy's Hospital, London, England

Health psychology is concerned with understanding human behaviour in the context of health and illness. The most widely used definition of the field has been provided by Matarazzo (1982), who described health psychology as the

> aggregate of specific educational, scientific, and professional contributions of the discipline of psychology to the promotion and maintenance of health, the prevention and treatment of illness, and the identification of etiologic and diagnostic correlates of health, illness, and related dysfunction. (p. 4)

Thus health psychologists study the psychological factors that influence how people stay healthy, why they become ill, and how they respond to illness and treatment. This chapter will overview each of these areas to illustrate the breadth and variety of work.

As with many other areas of psychology, there are three types of health

76

psychology research, namely descriptive, explanatory, and intervention-based. Although a great deal of current research is descriptive, there are increasing attempts to develop explanatory approaches. For example, instead of providing a description of a health-related behaviour (e.g., dietary choice; adhering to medication) and perhaps relating it to an outcome (e.g., health status), more studies are using models to explain health-related behaviours or to predict their outcomes. The development of models is obviously import-ant in any field since they add strength to the design and interpretation of research. For this reason, a separate section is included on a selection of widely used models of health-related behaviour.

THE EMERGENCE OF HEALTH PSYCHOLOGY

Health psychology emerged as a separate discipline in the 1970s, and there are many reasons for this and for its rapid development. An important back-ground factor is the major change in the nature of health problems in indus-trialized societies during the twentieth century. Until the 1900s, the primary causes of illness and death were pneumonia, influenza, tuberculosis, and other infectious diseases. Since that time, chronic illnesses such as heart disease and cancer have become the leading causes of death (see Table 1). These are diseases for which social and psychological factors have been shown to be important as causal agents and in determining how individuals cope with the diseases and respond to their treatment. The provision of health care has

Table 1 The changes in leading causes of death in the USA, 1900–1980

Cause of death	1900	1980
Pneumonia/influenza	1	6
TB	2	
Diarrhoea and other gastro-intestinal disease	3	
Heart disease	4	1
Intra-cranial vascular lesions	5	
Nephritis	6	
Accidents	7	4
Cancer	8	2
Senility	9	
Diphtheria	10	
Diabetes		7
Cardiovascular disease		3
Chronic obstructive pulmonary disease		5
Cirrhosis of the liver		8
Atherosclerosis		9
Suicide		10

Source: Based on Matarazzo and Leckliter, 1988

grown enormously and there is an increased emphasis on good communication as a central ingredient of medical treatment, an awareness of the importance of patient satisfaction and of quality of life as a key outcome in evaluating the efficacy of medical interventions (Fallowfield, 1990).

In view of all these changes, there has been a shift from an exclusively biomedical model of health towards a much broader "biopsychosocial" one (Engel, 1977). Whereas the biomedical approach reduces the explanation of illness to biological malfunction, a biopsychosocial approach recognizes the complex, multifactorial nature of illness causation and outcome, as well as the concept of health as a positive state (i.e., not merely the absence of illness). Similarly, whereas biomedical treatments will typically involve physical methods (e.g., medication, surgery, etc.) to reduce or eliminate physical symptoms, health psychology shows us not only that it is possible to use psychological approaches to prevention and treatment but also that the efficacy of any treatment depends on a variety of psychological and social factors, including the quality of the relationship between practitioner and patient. Moreover, the important criteria for judging treatment success not only may be in terms of changes in physical symptoms but also will be reflected in psychological and social outcomes such as coping, mood, and quality or life (see Kaplan, 1990).

BEHAVIOURAL FACTORS INFLUENCING HEALTH

A wide range of behaviours can influence health. In broad terms these have been classified in positive and negative terms as health-protective or health-risk behaviours, and many of these are described later in the chapter (see below, on lifestyle and health). Risk-increasing behaviours have been referred to as *behavioural pathogens*, whereas health-enhancing or protective behaviours have been referred to as *behavioural immunogens* (see Matarazzo & Leckliter, 1988). The influence of these behaviours on health has been established from epidemiological studies of populations which examine the factors associated with the incidence of different diseases. Thus they reflect a statistical correlation and do not necessarily show how or why the behaviour concerned has an effect on health status. We begin with an overview of a number of different behavioural factors that affect health. First, there is a focus on the topic of stress and its effects. There is then a consideration of personality factors that can influence health and health behaviour. Finally, there is an outline of so-called "lifestyle" factors that can have both positive and negative health consequences.

Stress and health

The links between stress, health, and disease are complex and need to be examined carefully. Stress is usually used to describe situations in which

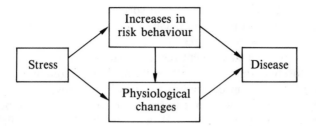

Figure 1 Stress and disease: direct and indirect effects

individuals are faced with demands that exceed their immediate ability to cope (Lazarus & Folkman, 1984). Stressful situations are typically those that are novel, unpredictable, and uncontrollable as well as those involving change or loss. Very often, these situations produce adverse psychological and physiological changes which, in turn, may result in disease.

However, a major problem for health psychologists is to understand the way in which stress is associated with the development of illness. Two broad possibilities have been proposed; these have been referred to as "indirect" and "direct" effects (see Figure 1). Thus stress may have indirect effects on health by increasing levels of risk behaviour (e.g., smoking, alcohol consumption), or may have direct effects on specific physiological mechanisms (e.g., increases in blood pressure) as well as affecting the individual's resistance to disease through suppression of the immune system, or by exacerbating or triggering a disease process in an already vulnerable individual.

A range of behavioural responses are shown by individuals as they attempt to cope with stressful situations and the associated emotions. At the same time there are neuroendocrine and immunological changes resulting from acute or chronic stressful episodes. During stressful episodes, releasing factors from the brain cause the pituitary to release adrenocorticotropic hormone (ACTH) which gives rise to the release of corticosteroids from the cortex of the adrenal glands. In addition to producing a number of well-known changes associated with the mobilization of both short and longer-term physical resources (e.g., release of adrenalin or noradrenaline; release of glucose; activation of endorphins/encephalins; etc.), these steroids can also have effects on the immune system. Thus fairly acute stressors, such as exams, and more chronic stressors, such as caring for a dependent elderly relative, can lead to deleterious immunological changes and increased incidence of illness (see Kiecolt-Glaser & Glaser, 1987).

Personality and health

Older studies attempting to link psychological factors with specific diseases gave rise to the rather misleading idea that different types of diseases are experienced by individuals with certain sorts of personality. In general this research, often based on psychodynamic theories and the idea that certain sorts of subconscious conflict result in specific patterns of disease, has not received support from subsequent research. However, there is growing evidence from different, more credible sources, that personality can influence health and play a role in determining illness in other ways.

Probably the best known work in this area concerns the link between the so-called "Type A" personality and coronary heart disease (Friedman & Rosenman, 1974). The Type A personality was characterized by competitiveness, time urgency, hostility, and related behavioural factors which were associated with a significantly increased risk of coronary heart disease. Although the earlier studies in the 1960s and 1970s were very encouraging, subsequent work has complicated the picture. Some studies have notably failed to find any relation between Type A and heart disease; it is now thought that only certain components (e.g., anger and hostility) of the original Type A formulation are "pathogenic".

How is the Type A behaviour pattern associated with increased levels of heart disease? As was discussed above, there are almost certainly direct and indirect effects of Type A behaviour on health. Type A individuals show a greater physiological reactivity (e.g., in blood pressure and heart-rate) to environmental demands and may even generate more demands by their style of behaviour. Thus the more frequent elevations in blood pressure and higher levels of hormonal change linked to stress responses may eventually cause adverse physical changes to the heart and blood vessels. Also, Type A individuals are more likely to engage in unhealthy behaviours since they drink more alcohol than Type B individuals and, if they smoke, they inhale their cigarette smoke for a longer time. They are less likely to relax and more often push themselves to their physical limits.

Type A behaviour is the most extensively investigated personality factor in current health psychology research, and there have been impressive interventions developed to change the behaviour pattern, with positive health outcomes (see Thoresen, Friedman, Powell, Gill, & Ulmer, 1985). However there is other research investigating personality in relation to disease-proneness and to health behaviours. For example Temoshok and colleagues have investigated the role of Type C personality in relation to cancer (Temoshok, 1987). The Type C personality is characterized by a difficulty in the expression of emotion and by the tendency to suppress or inhibit emotions, particularly negative emotions such as anger. Some psychologists have proposed that these aspects of personality can play a causal role in cancer but, as yet, there are no convincing data on this (see Fox, 1988). However, there are clearer indications that these kinds of factors may influence the progression of cancer and hence the survival time of individuals with cancer. Currently, interventions that encourage positive patterns of responding emotionally are being evaluated in cancer patients and it remains to be seen whether these can be effective.

Personality variables can influence health in a variety of ways, and a broad distinction can be made between those with a positive relation to health and health behaviour and those with an adverse relation. In contrast to the adverse effects of Type A and Type C, other personality variables can be protective in various ways. One which has generated a great deal of interest is the concept of *hardiness* (Kobasa, 1979) which describes individuals with a high sense of personal control over events in their lives, with a strong sense of commitment or involvement, together with a tendency to see environmental demands or changes as challenges.

Hardy individuals are thought to be less affected by stress: there is some evidence for this, even though there are problems in measuring hardiness. Other related aspects of personality have also shown to be health-protective. One example is that of *optimism* (Scheier, Weintraub, & Carver, 1986) which describes a tendency towards positive expectations in life and which enables individuals to cope better with stressors and engage in healthier lifestyles.

Finally, there is emerging evidence that general patterns of positive or negative emotional responses, associated with personality, can influence various aspects of health (Watson & Pennebaker, 1991). Individuals who are high in negative affect (i.e., experience more negative emotions, particularly anxiety) do not seem to be more prone to disease, but they are more likely to notice bodily changes and symptoms and consequently seek medical help more frequently. In contrast, those individuals high in positive affect, as reflected by a more engaged and enthusiastic approach to life, are less likely to report health problems or to seek medical help. Watson and Pennebaker provide interesting evidence to indicate that these styles of emotional responding are very much personality-related and may possibly be genetically determined.

The role of personality factors in health is obviously complex (see Friedman & Booth-Kewley, 1987). Older ideas about particular patterns of personality and emotional conflict being associated with particular diseases have not been supported. However, there is important evidence that aspects of personality may make individuals more or less vulnerable to the effects of stress and can influence both health and illness behaviours.

Lifestyle and health

One very obvious way in which behaviour can influence health comes from research on lifestyle, which has identified a number of behaviours that can have both positive and negative effects on health status. The word "lifestyle" is usually applied to the coherent and consistent use of a range of different health behaviours (Nutbeam, Aaro, & Wold, 1991). However, individuals are not always entirely consistent across different health behaviours, and so we

81

shall focus on separate behaviours and their effects on health rather than on the more generic concept of lifestyle.

The effects on health of behaviours such as smoking and high alcohol use are well documented. There is overwhelming evidence that smokers not only are much more likely to die from lung cancer and other cancers but also have much higher rates of cardiovascular disease and chronic respiratory disorders, particularly emphysema and chronic bronchitis. Moreover the disease risk is dose-related in that higher levels of smoking are more strongly associated with all these diseases. With sustained high levels of alcohol use a different but equally unpleasant spectrum of health problems can be seen. Drinking is a major cause of accidents particularly motoring accidents and can cause liver damage as well as having detrimental effects on brain functioning.

For health psychologists, the key questions about health-risk behaviours concern their origin, their maintenance, and their prevention or treatment. There are diverse determinants of both behaviours since both may start as ways of coping with stress, in response to peer pressure, for pleasure, and for a number of other reasons. Similarly, they will be maintained by a variety of psychological, social, and biological factors. Even though their effects on health are physical and dramatic it is nevertheless important to remember that they are behaviours and that the routes to limiting their effects are through prevention and behaviour change.

There are many other risky behaviours that cannot be discussed in detail in an overview; these include drug abuse, poor diet, and accidents, and the health effects of all these are also well documented. Although health psychology has an important role to play in describing, explaining, and intervening in all risk behaviours, it is very important not to think of these problems exclusively in individual, behavioural terms since they often reflect adverse social circumstances or particular cultural contexts.

The same caveats about the influence of social and cultural factors must also be applied to the understanding of health-protective or health-enhancing behaviours. The behavioural factors (seven or eight hours' sleep; eating three regular meals each day, including breakfast; moderate body weight; not smoking; limited alcohol intake; regular physical activity) identified by the Alameda County study (Breslow & Enstrom, 1980) provide some indicators of basic behaviours that can have a positive (or negative) influence on health. This study showed that the adoption of all or most of these health practices was associated with significantly lower mortality in the following five- and ten-year follow-up periods.

There is now a growing body of evidence to indicate that regular exercise has a beneficial effect on physical and psychological health (Haskell, 1984). Exercise can reduce the incidence of physical health problems in elderly people and facilitate recovery from heart attack. However, there can be significant problems in ensuring that exercise and other health-promoting activities are adhered to (Dishman, 1982). Thus interventions need to be carefully planned and delivered by appropriately skilled individuals since it has been found to be extremely hard to give up risky behaviours and to adopt more healthy lifestyles. Providing information is usually insufficient to promote change, since it is necessary to alter cognitions (see below, on explaining health behaviour) and to influence social networks as a basis for bringing about changes in health-related behaviour.

PSYCHOLOGICAL ASPECTS OF ILLNESS AND HEALTH CARE

Coping and social support

There is now a great deal of interest in the way patients respond to chronic illness. Much of this work has been concerned with understanding the way patients cope with the different demands of their illnesses. Whereas older work assumed that the demands depended primarily on the illness, more recent studies show that coping depends very much on the individual's perception of the threats and demands as well as on the social circumstances in which the illness is experienced (Burish & Bradley, 1983).

Coping is a general term that describes the wide range of responses used by individuals to deal with their health problems. Although the concept of coping seems straightforward, there is still disagreement about its nature and measurement as well as about its effects on emotional and physical outcomes (Cohen, 1987). It is generally agreed that coping is not a static process in the context of chronic illness since it can change over time as the perceptions, demands, and social implications of the illness change. Some researchers prefer to use very broad dimensions of behaviour (e.g., approach vs avoidance) to characterize individual differences in coping behaviour, whereas others focus on much more specific behaviours in order to describe the wide range of responses shown by patients. It is also unclear whether coping determines psychological or physical well-being or whether this relationship is a more two-way process. A great deal of the coping research has been based on the assumption that coping determines various outcomes, such as emotional state, but there are increasing indications that coping can also be a consequence of emotional state (Fillip, Kauer, Freudenberg, & Ferring, 1990).

The individual's social circumstances are also of particular importance in determining the way in which patients cope and in the degree of success that coping strategies can have in regulating their well-being. The most widely used concept here is that of *social support* which refers not only to the access one has to other individuals but also to their perceived value or adequacy in actually providing support. As with coping, there are conceptual and methodological issues associated with social support. Social support does not always produce a beneficial outcome (see Schwarzer & Leppin, 1989) and it is important to understand the relationship between different types and sources of support and different physical and psychological outcomes for the patient. Nevertheless, social support can have significant direct and indirect effects on the well-being of individuals with chronic illnesses and disabilities. Thus those individuals with little or no effective social support are more likely to show a poorer response to illness or treatment.

The increasing understanding of the nature and role of such processes as coping and social support are particularly important for developing interventions in this area. General training for health professionals in communication and listening skills (see below) can provide a basis for understanding more about patients' needs. More specific psychological interventions have been developed for helping patients cope better with certain aspects of their illness. There is now a range of psychological approaches for the management of chronic pain which is a very common component of chronic or disabling conditions (Pearce & Erskine, 1989).

Communication

Many studies have examined aspects of communication between health-care professionals (HCPs), particularly doctors and patients, in order to explain the all-too-often disappointing outcomes (see Ley, 1988). These have shown that patients complain frequently that they are not given sufficient information or that their doctors do not seem interested or concerned. Moreover, it has been found that patients may find it difficult to understand or remember information that they have been given. Not surprisingly therefore, there is quite widespread evidence of patient dissatisfaction with communication.

A number of problems have been described in the outcomes of medical encounters and, of these, the two most widely investigated have been the low levels of patient satisfaction and the low rates of adherence to advice or treatment (see below). Causes of these problems are quite diverse but many relate to aspects of the communication process and the failure of the HCP to attend to and discuss the needs and concerns of the patient. This has led to a number of psychological interventions in this area, including communication skills training for HCPs, particularly during their early training (Weinman & Armstrong, 1988). Some of these training interventions have aimed to improve general communication skills, whereas others have been designed for work with particular types of patients or particular situations (e.g., giving "bad news").

Adherence to treatment

The term "adherence" describes the extent to which an individual follows recommended treatment or advice. Older studies tended to use the term "compliance" but adherence is now preferred for a number of reasons. It refers to a broad range of behaviours including taking medication and following advice about health-related behaviour change such as dietary change, quitting smoking, or increasing levels of exercise. Thus adherence can be seen as a potentially health-enhancing behaviour, but more typically non-adherence or low adherence is a potential health-risk behaviour.

High levels of non-adherence have been found across a range of treatments and treatment settings (Meichenbaum & Turk, 1987). Very typically, findings are that some 40–50 per cent of patients do not adhere to treatment or advice in a way that is clinically significant. The level of adherence is affected by treatment and illness factors, since the lowest rates of adherence are found in patients with chronic conditions and in those taking medication for preventive purposes. In contrast, patients receiving such treatments as chemotherapy for cancer generally show very high levels of adherence, even though the treatments may produce unpleasant side-effects.

Although factors associated with the nature of the illness and the demands of the treatment influence patient adherence, many studies have also identified the contribution of communication and patients' beliefs. The quality of communication between doctor and patient has a strong influence on patient satisfaction, which in turn plays a role in determining adherence levels. As was discussed earlier, quality of communication depends not only on the doctor's ability to listen and respond effectively to the patient's problems, but also on the way information is presented.

Much early work on adherence pointed to the importance of the health beliefs (described below). If patients perceive their condition as serious and believe in the efficacy of the treatment, they are more likely to adhere to it. For adherence to recommendations to avoid or reduce health-risk behaviours such as smoking, or to adopt potentially health-protective behaviours such as "safe sex" practices, there is increasing evidence that "normative beliefs" are particularly important. These are the beliefs held by individuals about the views or attitudes held by their social peers.

Health psychologists have devised a variety of interventions to facilitate adherence (see Meichenbaum & Turk, 1987). Some of these are based on communication training for health professionals in order to improve their basic communication skills including their ability to present information concerning treatment. More focused interventions encourage the doctor to share decision-making and treatment planning with the patient in order to agree treatment goals and anticipate any barriers.

Psychological responses to investigations and treatments

Many studies have demonstrated the stressfulness associated with admission to hospital and with various medical investigative or treatment procedures. As a result, psychologists have provided a range of interventions to prepare patients for hospitalization generally, or for a specific unpleasant procedure within the hospital setting. Preparation for hospital admission has mostly been confined to work with children (Eiser, 1988), but preparations for stressful procedures have been developed for both children and adults. These interventions work at a number of levels. Some essentially provide information as to what will happen to the patient, in terms of the nature of the procedure and its likely effects. Others are designed to reduce anxiety, either generally using relaxation training or by helping the patient to identify and cope with specific fears or concerns. For children there are videotapes of other children undergoing the same investigations or treatment: these allow children to model themselves on the child in the video.

The interventions have had a mixed success in helping patients cope with the procedures and in improving the outcome (Weinman & Johnston, 1988). There are many different sorts of outcome that can be affected (e.g., pain, anxiety, speed of recovery, etc.) and some interventions are clearly better for achieving particular outcomes. Overall it would appear that cognitive-behavioural approaches produce better outcomes than other types of interventions on both behavioural and self-report measures. It may also be necessary to match the type of intervention to the patient's coping style and informational needs.

Health psychologists have also been concerned with understanding how health-care professionals are affected by their work environment. There are widespread reports of job stress among HCPs and a number of factors appear to contribute to this. These include the stressfulness of the work, the lack of support, and the working conditions and long hours worked by many HCPs (Herbert, 1990). As a result various psychological interventions have been developed for the management of job stress in HCPs (Sutherland, 1990).

EXPLAINING HEALTH-RELATED BEHAVIOUR: SOCIAL-COGNITIVE APPROACHES

We shall now outline some models and approaches that are concerned with the cognition (beliefs, attitudes, perceptions, etc.) underlying health-related behaviours. At present, these are the most widely used explanatory models and frameworks in health psychology and have been applied as explanations of health-risk behaviours (e.g., Croog & Richards, 1977), preventive or protective behaviours, and in explaining differential responses to stress. They are also used to explain the nature of psychological responses to illness (e.g., Affleck, Tennen, Croog, & Levine, 1987) and the extent of behaviours such as adherence to medication or recommended lifestyle change (e.g., Meichenbaum & Turk, 1987). Despite their popularity, these models still do not provide complete explanations of specific health or illness behaviours. This may partly be because they were not all originally developed to explain health-related behaviours and may not reflect the ways that individuals think about their own health or illness. It may also be because many aspects of health are determined or shaped by social and cultural factors (see Blaxter, 1990) as well as individual cognitions.

Specific models of health-related behaviour

The most established model of health-related behaviour is the *Health Belief Model* (HBM: Janz & Becker, 1984), which proposes that, in response to a cue or action, such as the experience of a symptom or invitation to attend a health check, individuals will act on the basis of their beliefs about the threat of a potential health problem, as well as their beliefs about the advantages and disadvantages of taking a particular course of action. Their perception of the threat will depend on their beliefs about its seriousness and their susceptibility or vulnerability to it.

Thus for individuals to engage in a specific health-related behaviour (e.g., "safe" sexual behaviour), they must consider not only that they may be vulnerable to the possible consequences of not engaging in that behaviour (being infected by HIV) but also that the consequences are serious. Moreover they need to believe that the advantages of engaging in that behaviour outweigh the disadvantages of doing so. Thus for some health-related behaviours (e.g., "safe" sexual behaviour) individuals may acknowledge the seriousness of the associated health threat but may not see themselves as being vulnerable. In contrast, for behaviours such as dental health care, individuals may well acknowledge their susceptibility to the health threat (caries or gum disease) but may not regard it as sufficiently serious to take the appropriate preventive action.

The HBM has been extensively used for studies of health-related behaviour, particularly those concerned with prevention. It has not been entirely successful and, as a result, other variables (e.g., efficacy beliefs – see below) have been added to increase its explanatory power. Even with these, the overall results are still quite modest; this may partly reflect the general problem of trying to predict behaviour from attitudes, as well as the more specific problem that people may not necessarily think about health issues in the way suggested by the HBM.

A less widely used but more successful model is the *Theory of Reasoned Action* (TRA: Ajzen & Fishbein, 1980), which proposes that the best predictors of individuals' voluntary actions are their behavioural *intentions*, which are determined by two factors. The first is their *attitude* regarding the behaviour; this is based on two types of *behavioural beliefs* – beliefs about the likely outcomes of behaviour (e.g., "If I exercise, I will improve my health") and evaluations of these outcomes (e.g., "Being healthy is important to me"). The second determinant of intentions is the *subjective norm* concerning the behaviour, which is based on two *normative beliefs* – beliefs regarding others' opinions about the behaviour (e.g., "My family and friends think I should exercise") and the motivation to comply with these opinions (e.g., "I wish to do what they want").

The TRA proposes that the subjective norm and attitude regarding the behaviour combine to produce an intention, which leads to performance of the behaviour. The theory has been developed as the *Theory of Planned Behaviour* (Ajzen, 1985) which adds other variables, including perceived behavioural control and perceived barriers.

Both the HBM and the TRA conceptualize health-related behaviour as a rational process based on the interplay and weighing up of organized beliefs. Unfortunately, health behaviours may not be like this in all individuals since some may occur for reasons other than health. For example, dieting or good dental hygiene may be carried out for primarily cosmetic reasons rather than for avoiding long-term health consequences. Also, specific health beliefs are far more likely to be useful in predicting health behaviours in those who attach a high value to health (Lau, Hartman, & Ware, 1986). Thus the concept of health value and the relative priority given to health in comparison with other factors (e.g., wealth, happiness, appearance, etc.) is an important general cognitive variable to take account of in explaining health behaviours.

Perceptions of cause and control

An individual's motivation or willingness to engage in a health-related behaviour not only depends on beliefs about the health issue concerned but also will be influenced by a belief in the ability to carry out the behaviour concerned. This has been referred to as a self-efficacy expectancy or belief and has been proposed by Bandura (1986) as a key determinant of all behaviour including health-behaviour. Bandura has developed a general theory of behaviour change which distinguishes two important related beliefs: *self-efficacy*, which refers to the belief that an individual can succeed at a particular task or with a particular behaviour (e.g., giving up smoking); and *outcome efficacy*, which refers to the belief that the behaviour will result in a valued outcome (e.g., that the treatment will be successful).

Self-efficacy beliefs are based on the previous experiences of individuals and on their observations of the behaviour of others in equivalent situations. Individuals with a high level of self-efficacy will probably attribute previous successes to their own efforts or abilities rather than to the help of others or to chance factors. Similarly, they will be more likely to have a high *internal locus of control* belief. Both of these concepts (attributions, locus of control) are also used to explain health and illness behaviours.

The concept of *health locus of control* has been developed by Wallston, Wallston, South, and Dobbins (Wallston et al., 1987) and identifies three distinct sources of control over health behaviours, namely self (internal control), powerful others (doctors, etc.), and chance factors. In general those with high internal locus of control beliefs are more likely to carry out preventive and other health actions. However, it is usually necessary to specify the type of health-behaviour (e.g., control over diabetes) in order for these control beliefs to be useful as predictors.

Attribution theory (see Turnquist, Harvey, & Anderson, 1988) is concerned with people's explanations for events and has shown that these can be described in terms of a number of important dimensions (due to oneself or external factors, due to a temporary or more long-lasting factor: due to a specific or a more global cause; etc.). The types of causal attributions that people make for illnesses and accidents have been found to influence their subsequent adjustment and psychological well-being (e.g., Affleck et al., 1987).

Attribution theory has also been used to describe more long-term or personality-related aspects of causal thinking. These are referred to as attributional styles and they assume that people show a consistency in the types of attributions they make over time and in different situations. This has been mainly applied to the study of the role of cognitions in depression (Peterson & Seligman, 1984) but later work suggests the possibility of attributional styles in the perception of symptoms (Robbins & Kirmayer, 1991).

Illness representation models (Lau, Bernard, & Hartman, 1989; Meyer, Leventhal, & Guttman, 1985) are concerned with the way patients conceptualize or make sense of illness or health threats. Leventhal and colleagues propose that there are three stages which regulate the adaptive behaviours during an illness (Meyer et al., 1985). The stages are cognitive representation, action planning or coping, and appraisal. The first involves the individual developing a model or representation of what is going wrong and of the causes and consequences of this. The second stage involves plans to deal with the problem; the efficacy of these is evaluated during the third stage, which in turn may result in changes in the representation and/or in the coping plans.

Five components of illness representations have been identified:

1 *Identity* which comprises both an abstract label (e.g., hypertension) as well as concrete signs and symptoms that are experienced or associated. This is very much the individual's own idea as what the disease is.
2 *Consequences* the individual's ideas about the short-term and longer-term consequences of the disease.
3 *Time-line* the individual's perceived time-frame for the development and duration of the disease or health threat. Typically illnesses are initially thought of as having an acute or short-term time-line, and it may take considerable time before the chronicity of a condition is accurately understood.
4 *Causes* the perceived causes of the disease (see above, on attribution theory).
5 *Cure* the individual's ideas about the possibilities of cures and their likely impact.

Although research in this area is still at an early stage, it has shown that many responses to illness (e,g., the type of coping, adherence to medication) are determined by the individual's own representation or understanding of the illness (see Skelton & Croyle, 1991).

CONCLUSIONS

This selective overview of health psychology has attempted to demonstrate the range of psychological processes in health and health care. At the present time, it is a disciplinary area of psychology with an emphasis on research into health and illness behaviour. However, many interventions have been developed for healthy individuals, patients, and health-care staff. Thus there is a very important practitioner component to health psychology, and this may well result in specific professional developments in the near future. In the USA, professional postgraduate training in health psychology is developing quite rapidly; in other countries (e.g., Canada, The Netherlands, and the United Kingdom) postgraduate programmes began to emerge in the early 1990s (see Jansen & Weinman, 1991).

Health psychology has established itself very rapidly but still has a long way to go. Future research must provide greater insights into the ways in which psychological processes can influence the biological mechanisms in health and disease. Also, a much clearer understanding and better theoretical models are needed for all aspects of health and illness behaviour. All this will inevitably result in the more widespread use of psychological interventions for preventing and treating health problems, and for the effective delivery of health care.

FURTHER READING

Bennett, P., Weinman, J., & Spurgeon, P. (Eds) (1990). *Current developments in health psychology*. London: Harwood Academic.

Gatchel, R. J., Baum, A., & Krantz, D. (1989). *An Introduction to health psychology* (2nd edn). New York: Random House.

Sarafino, E. P. (1990). *Health psychology: Biopsychosocial interactions*. New York: Wiley.

Taylor, S. E. (1990). *Health psychology* (2nd edn). New York: Random House.

REFERENCES

Affleck, G., Tennen, H., Croog, S., & Levine, S. (1987). Causal attribution, perceived control and recovery from a heart attack. *Journal of Social and Clinical Psychology*, 5, 356–364.

Ajzen, I. (1985). *From intentions to actions: A theory of planned behavior*. Englewood Cliffs, NJ: Prentice-Hall.

Ajzen, I., & Fishbein, M. (1980). *Understanding attitudes and predicting social behavior*. Englewood Cliffs, NJ: Prentice-Hall.

Bandura, A. (1986). *Social foundations of thought and action: Social cognitive theory*. Englewood Cliffs, NJ: Prentice-Hall.

Blaxter, M. (1990). *Health and lifestyle*. London: Tavistock.

Breslow, L., & Enstrom, J. (1980). Persistence of health habits and their relationship to mortality. *Preventive Medicine*, 9, 469–483.

Burish, T. C., & Bradley, L. A. (Eds) (1983). *Coping with chronic disease: Research and applications*. New York: Academic Press.

Cohen, F. (1987). Measurement of coping. In S. V. Kasl & C. L. Cooper (Eds) *Stress and health: Issues in research methodology* (pp. 283–305). Chichester: Wiley.

Croog, S., & Richards, N. P. (1977). Health beliefs and smoking patterns in heart patients and their wives: A longitudinal study. *American Journal of Public Health*, 67, 921–993.

Dishman, R. K. (1982). Compliance/adherence in health-related exercise. *Health Psychology*, 1, 237–267.

Eiser, C. (1988). Do children benefit from psychological preparation for hospitalisation? *Psychology and Health*, 2, 107–132.

Engel, G. L. (1977). The need for a new medical model: A challenge for biomedicine. *Science*, 196, 129–136.

Fallowfield, L. (1990). *The quality of life: The missing measurement in health care*. London: Souvenir.

Fillip, S.-H., Kauer, T., Freudenberg, E., & Ferring, D. (1990). The regulation of subjective well-being in cancer patients: An analysis of coping effectiveness. *Psychology and Health*, 4, 305–318.

Fox, B. H. (1988). Psychogenic factors in cancer, especially its incidence. In S. Maes, C. D. Spielberger, P. B. Defares, & I. G. Sarason (Eds) *Topics in health psychology* (pp. 37–55). Chichester: Wiley.

Friedman, H. S., & Booth-Kewley, S. (1987). The disease-prone personality: A meta-analytic view of the construct. *American Psychologist*, 42(6), 539–555.

Friedman, M., & Rosenman, R. H. (1974). *Type A behaviour and your heart*. New York: Knopf.

Haskell, W. L. (1984). Overview: Health benefits of exercise. In J. D. Matarazzo, S. M. Weiss, J. A. Herd, N. E. Miller, & S. M. Weiss (Eds) *Behavioral Health* (pp. 409–423). New York: Wiley.

Herbert, M. (1990). Healthcare workers in adverse environments. In P. Bennett, J. Weinman, & P. Spurgeon (Eds) *Current developments in health psychology* (pp. 277–304). London: Harwood Academic.

Jansen, M., & Weinman, J. (Eds) (1991). *The international development of health psychology*. London: Harwood Academic.

Janz, N. K., & Becker, M. (1984). The health belief model: A decade later. *Health Education Quarterly*, 11, 1–47.

Kaplan, R. M. (1990). Behavior as the central outcome in health care. *American Psychologist*, 45(11), 1211–1220.

Kiecolt-Glaser, J. K., & Glazer, R. (1987). Psychological moderators of immune function. *Annals of Behavioural Medicine*, 9(2), 16–20.

Kobasa, S. C. (1979). Stressful events and health: An enquiry into hardiness. *Journal of Personality and Social Psychology*, 37, 1–11.

Lau, R. R., Bernard, T. M., & Hartman, K. A. (1989). Further explorations of common sense representations of common illnesses. *Health Psychology*, 8, 195–219.

Lau, R. R., Hartman, K. A. & Ware, J. E. (1986). Health as value: Methodological and theoretical considerations. *Health Psychology*, 5, 25–43.

Lazarus, R. S., & Folkman, S. (1984). *Stress, appraisal and coping*. New York: Springer.

Ley, P. (1988). *Communicating with patients: Improving communication, satisfaction and compliance*. London: Croom Helm.

Matarazzo, J. D. (1982). Behavioral health's challenge to academic, scientific and professional psychology. *American Psychologist, 37*, 1–14.

Matarazzo, J. D., & Leckliter, I. N. (1988). Behavioral health: The role of good and bad habits in health and illness. In S. Maes, C. D. Spielberger, P. B. Defares, & I. G. Sarason (Eds) *Topics in health psychology* (pp. 3–18). Chichester: Wiley.

Meichenbaum, D., & Turk, D. C. (1987). *Facilitating treatment adherence: A practitioner's guidebook*. New York: Plenum.

Meyer, D., Leventhal, H., & Guttman, M. (1985). Common-sense models of illness: The example of hypertension. *Health Psychology, 4*, 115–135.

Nutbeam, D., Aaro, L., & Wold, B. (1991). The lifestyle concept and health education for young people. *World Health Statistics Quarterly, 44*, 55–61.

Pearce, S., & Erskine, A. (1989). Chronic pain. In S. Pearce & J. Wardle (Eds) *The practice of behavioural medicine* (pp. 427–442). Oxford: Oxford University Press.

Peterson, C., & Seligman, M. E. P. (1984). Causal explanations as a risk factor for depression: Theory and evidence. *Psychological Review, 91*, 347–374.

Robbins, J. M., & Kirmayer, L. J. (1991). Attributions of common somatic symptoms. *Psychological Medicine, 21*, 1029–1045.

Scheier, M. F., Weintraub, J. K., & Carver, C. S. (1986). Coping with stress: Divergent strategies of optimists and pessimists. *Journal of Personality and Social Psychology, 51*, 1257–1264.

Schwarzer, R., & Leppin, A. (1989). Social support and health: A meta-analysis. *Psychology and Health, 3*, 1–16.

Skelton, J. A., & Croyle, R. T. (Eds) (1991). *Mental representation in health and illness*. New York: Springer-Verlag.

Stone, G. C., Weiss, S. M., & Matarazzo, J. D. (Eds) (1987). *Health psychology: A discipline and a profession*. Chicago, IL: University of Chicago Press.

Sutherland, V. (1990) . Managing stress at the worksite. In P. Bennett, J. Weinman, & P. Spurgeon (Eds) *Current developments in health psychology* (pp. 305–330). London: Harwood Academic.

Temoshok, L. (1987). Personality, copying style, emotions and cancer: Towards an integrative model. *Cancer Surveys, 6*, 545–567.

Thoresen, C., Friedman, M., Powell, L. H., Gill, J. J., & Ulmer, D. (1985). Altering the Type A behavior pattern in postinfarction patients. *Journal of Cardiopulmonary Rehabilitation, 5*, 258–266.

Turnquist, D. C., Harvey, J. H., & Anderson, B. L. (1988). Attributions and adjustment to life-threatening disease. *British Journal of Clinical Psychology, 27*, 55–65.

Wallston, K. A., Wallston, B. S., South, S., & Dobbins, C. J. (1987). Perceived control and health. *Current Psychological Research and Reviews, 6*, 5–25.

Watson, D., & Pennebaker, J. W. (1991). Situational, dispositional and genetic bases of symptom reporting. In J. A. Skelton & R. T. Croyle (Eds) *Mental representation in health and illness* (pp. 60–84). New York: Springer-Verlag.

Weinman, J., & Armstrong, D. (1988). Using interview training as a preparation for behavioural science teaching. In J. Aldridge-Smith, A. Butler, H. Dent, & R. H. S. Mindham (Eds) *Proceedings of first conference of behavioural sciences in medical undergraduate education* (pp. 20–29). Leeds: Leeds University Press.

Weinman, J., & Johnston, M. (1988). Stressful medical procedures: An analysis of the effects of psychological interventions and of the stressfulness of the procedures. In S. Maes, C. D. Spielberger, P. B. Defares, & I. G. Sarason (Eds) *Topics in health psychology* (pp. 205–217). Chichester: Wiley.

GLOSSARY

This glossary is confined to a selection of frequently used terms that merit explanation or comment. Its informal definitions are intended as practical guides to meanings and usages. The entries are arranged alphabetically, word by word, and numerals are positioned as though they were spelled out.

acetylcholine one of the neurotransmitter (q.v.) substances that play a part in relaying information between neurons.

ACh a common abbreviation for acetylcholine (q.v.).

ACTH *see* adrenocorticotropic hormone (ACTH).

adolescence from the Latin *adolescere*, to grow up, the period of development between puberty and adulthood.

adrenal glands from the Latin *ad*, to, *renes*, kidneys, a pair of endocrine glands (q.v.), situated just above the kidneys, which secrete adrenalin (epinephrine), noradrenalin (norepinephrine) (qq.v.), and other hormones into the bloodstream. *See also* adrenocorticotropic hormone (ACTH).

adrenalin(e) hormone (q.v.) secreted by the adrenal glands (q.v.), causing an increase in blood pressure, release of sugar by the liver, and several other physiological reactions to perceived threat or danger. *See also* antidepressant drugs, endocrine glands, noradrenalin(e).

adrenocorticotropic hormone (ACTH) a hormone secreted by the pituitary gland that stimulates the adrenal gland to secrete corticosteroid hormones such as cortisol (hydrocortisone) into the bloodstream, especially in response to stress or injury.

altered state of consciousness (ASC) a state of consciousness induced by drugs, hypnosis, meditation, or other deliberate means that differs from ordinary wakefulness or sleep.

amnesia partial or complete loss of memory. Anterograde amnesia is loss of memory for events following the amnesia-causing trauma, or loss of the ability to form long-term memories for new facts and events; retrograde amnesia is loss of memory for events occurring shortly before the trauma.

analgesia, hypnotic insensitivity to pain in hypnosis (q.v.) resulting either from a direct suggestion that part of the body can feel no pain (suggested hypnotic analgesia) or from a suggestions that the subject's body or a part of it is not where it really is (spontaneous hypnotic analgesia).

androgynous from the Greek *andros*, man, *gyne*, woman, having both masculine and feminine qualities.

anterograde amnesia *see under* amnesia.

anti-anxiety drugs an umbrella term for a number of drugs, including the benzodiazepine drugs and the muscle relaxant meprobamate, that are used for reducing anxiety, also sometimes called minor tranquillizers.

93

antidepressant drugs drugs that influence neurotransmitters (q.v.) in the brain, used in the treatment of mood disorders (q.v.), especially depression. The monoamine oxidase inhibitor (MAOI) drugs block the absorption of amines such as dopamine, adrenalin, and noradrenalin (qq.v.), allowing these stimulants to accumulate at the synapses in the brain, the tricyclic antidepressants such as imipramine act by blocking the re-uptake of noradrenalin in particular, thereby similarly increasing its availability, and the selective serotonin re-uptake inhibitor fluoxetine hydrochloride (Prozac) blocks the re-uptake of serotonin (q.v.).

antipsychotic drugs a general terms for all drugs used to alleviate the symptoms of psychotic disorders. Major tranquillizers, including especially the phenothiazine derivatives such as chlorpromazine (Largactil) and thioridazine, are used primarily in the treatment of schizophrenia (q.v.) and other disorders involving psychotic symptoms; lithium compounds are used primarily in the treatment of bipolar (manic-depressive) disorder.

arousal a general term for an organism's state of physiological activation, mediated by the autonomic nervous system (q.v.). *See also* Yerkes-Dodson law.

attitude a fairly stable evaluative response towards a person, object, activity, or abstract concept, comprising a cognitive component (positive or negative perceptions and beliefs), an emotional component (positive or negative feelings), and a behavioural component (positive or negative response tendencies).

autonomic nervous system a subdivision of the nervous system (q.v.) that regulates (autonomously) the internal organs and glands. It is divided into the sympathetic nervous system and the parasympathetic nervous system (qq.v.).

barbiturates chemical compounds derived from barbituric acid, including barbitone and phenobarbitone, used as hypnotic or sedative drugs, liable to cause strong dependence when abused.

behavioural medicine an interdisciplinary field of study devoted to behavioural aspects of health and illness.

benzodiazepine drugs any of a group of chemical compounds that are used as anti-anxiety drugs (q.v.) and hypnotics (sleeping drugs), including diazepam (Valium) and chlordiazepoxide (Librium).

catecholamine any member of the group of hormones (q.v.) that are catechol derivatives, especially adrenalin, noradrenalin, and dopamine, (qq.v.), all of which are involved in the functioning of the nervous system.

central nervous system (CNS) in human beings and other vertebrates, the brain and spinal cord.

clairvoyance *see under* extrasensory perception (ESP).

CNS *see* central nervous system (CNS).

cognition from the Latin *cognoscere*, to know, attention, thinking, problem-solving, remembering, and all other mental processes that fall under the general heading of information processing.

cognitive interview a form of interview specially designed to elicit the maximum amount of reliable information from witnesses in forensic (criminological) psychology (q.v.), incorporating several memory enhancement features such as encouraging the interviewee to reinstate the context of the episode to be remembered and to recall the series of events in different sequences and from different perspectives.

correlation in statistics, the relationship between two variables such that high scores on one tend to go with high scores on the other or (in the case of negative correlation) such that high scores on one tend to go with low scores on the other. The usual index of correlation, called the product-moment correlation coefficient and symbolized by r, ranges from 1.00 for perfect positive correlation, through zero for uncorrelated variables, to -1.00 for perfect negative correlation.

cortisol *see under* adrenocorticotropic hormone (ACTH).

criminological psychology *see* forensic (criminological) psychology.

DA a common abbreviation for dopamine (q.v.).

déjà vu from the French for already seen, an illusion of having previously seen or experienced something that, in reality, one is seeing or experiencing for the first time. Analogous illusions are sometimes referred to as *déjà entendu* (already heard), *déjà pensé* (already thought), and so on.

delusion a false personal belief, maintained in the face of overwhelming contradictory evidence, excluding religious beliefs that are widely accepted by members of the person's culture or sub-culture, characteristic especially of delusional (paranoid) disorder (q.v.). *Cf.* hallucination.

delusional (paranoid) disorder formerly called paranoia, a mental disorder characterized by delusions (q.v.), especially of jealousy, grandeur, or persecution, but with otherwise unimpaired intellectual functioning.

demand characteristics features of an experimental situation that encourage certain types of behaviour from the subjects and can contaminate the results, especially when this behaviour arises from subjects' expectations or preconceptions or their interpretations of the experimenter's expectations. *Cf.* experimenter effects.

depersonalization a form of dissociation (q.v.) involving a feeling of loss of the sense of self, sometimes accompanied by an out-of-body experience (OBE) – a sense of perceiving oneself from a distance, usually from above – associated with sleep deprivation, some forms of drug intoxication, and various mental disorders including some forms of schizophrenia and dissociative disorder (qq.v.).

dissociation a process involving a group of psychological functions having a degree of unity among themselves which become detached from the rest of personality and function more or less independently, as in multiple personality disorder (q.v.).

dissociative disorder an umbrella term for psychological disorders, such as multiple personality disorder (q.v.) and the non-organic amnesias, involving dissociation (q.v.) and general disintegration of the functions of consciousness, self-concept, or perceptual-motor coordination.

dopamine a catecholamine (q.v.); one of the neurotransmitter (q.v.) substances significantly involved in central nervous, system functioning. *See also* antidepressant drugs.

DSM-IV the common name of the fourth edition of the *Diagnostic and Statistical Manual of Mental Disorders* of the American Psychiatric Association, published in 1994, replacing DSM-III-R, the revised version of the third edition published in 1987, containing the most authoritative classification and definitions of mental disorders (q.v.).

electrodermal response (EDR) *see* galvanic skin response (GSR).

emotion from the Latin *e*, away, *movere*, to move, any evaluative, affective, intentional, short-term psychological state.

endocrine gland any ductless gland, such as the adrenal gland or pituitary gland (qq.v.), that secretes hormones (q.v.) directly into the bloodstream. The endocrine system functions as an elaborate signalling system within the body, alongside the nervous system.

epinephrine, norepinephrine from the Greek *epi*, upon, *nephros*, kidney, alternative words for adrenalin and noradrenalin (qq.v.), especially in United States usage. *See also* endocrine gland.

experimenter bias *see* experimenter effects.

experimenter effects biasing effects on the results of an experiment caused by expectations or preconceptions on the part of the experimenter; also called experimenter bias. *Cf.* demand characteristics.

expert witness a witness in a court case whose function is to testify about matters beyond the knowledge and experience of a judge or jury and who, unlike an ordinary witness, is allowed to testify not only about facts but also about his or her opinions. Most expert psychological witnesses are either clinical or educational (school) psychologists.

extrasensory perception (ESP) in parapsychology (q.v.), perception supposedly occurring without the use of sense organs. Extrasensory perception of other people's thoughts is sometimes called telepathy, extrasensory perception of objects or events at a distance is called clairvoyance, and extrasensory perception of other people's future thoughts or of future events is called precognitive telepathy or clairvoyance, or simply precognition. The reality of all of these phenomena is highly controversial.

5-hydroxytryptamine (5-HT) another name for serotonin (q.v.).

forensic (criminological) psychology a branch of applied psychology concerned with all aspects of criminal behaviour and the application of psychology to practical problems of crime and punishment.

galvanic skin response (GSR) a fall in the resistance of the skin to the passage of a weak electric current, indicative of emotion or arousal, also called psychogalvanic response (PGR) and electrodermal response (EDR).

GSR *see* galvanic skin response (GSR).

hallucination from the Latin *alucinari*, to wander in the mind, a false perception (q.v.), most commonly visual or auditory, subjectively similar or identical to an ordinary perception but occurring in the absence of relevant sensory stimuli, characteristic in particular of some forms of schizophrenia (q.v.). False perceptions occurring during sleep, while falling asleep (hypnagogic image), or while awakening (hypnopompic image) are not normally considered to be hallucinations. *Cf.* delusion.

hallucinogenic drugs drugs such as lysergic acid diethylamide (LSD) or mescaline that induce hallucinations.

health psychology a branch of psychology concerned with psychological factors relevant to the promotion and maintenance of health, the prevention of illness, and the identification of psychological causes and correlates of health and illness.

hidden observer phenomenona phenomenon in hypnosis (q.v.) in which a part of the hypnotized subject's mind appears to be dissociated, so that although the subject's hand is hypnotically anaesthetized (for example), "some part" of him or her (the so-called hidden observer) can still feel pain in the hand.

hormone from the Greek *horman*, to stir up or urge on, a chemical substance secreted into the bloodstream by an endocrine gland (q.v.) and transported to another part of the body where it exerts a specific effect.

hypnagogic image *see under* hallucination.

hypnopompic image *see under* hallucination.

hypnosis from the Greek *hypnos*, sleep, an altered state of consciousness or a pattern of behaviour resembling such an altered state, characterized by apparently sleeplike

96

passivity, heightened responsiveness to suggestions from the hypnotist, narrowed attention, and various exotic phenomena.

imipramine *see under* antidepressant drugs.

lie detector *see under* polygraph.

locus of control in personality theory and social psychology, the perceived source of control over one's behaviour, on a scale from internal to external.

long-term memory (LTM) relatively long-lasting memory for information that has been deeply processed. *Cf.* sensory memory, short-term memory (STM).

memory the mental processes of encoding, storage, and retrieval of information. *See also* amnesia, long-term memory, short-term memory (STM).

mental disorder according to DSM-IV (q.v.), a psychological or behavioural syndrome or pattern associated with distress (a painful symptom), disability (impairment in one or more areas of functioning), and a significantly increased risk of death, pain, disability, or an important loss of freedom, occurring not merely as a predictable response to a disturbing life-event.

monoamine oxidase inhibitor (MAOI) *see under* antidepressant drugs.

mood disorders a group of mental disorders characterized by disturbances of affect or mood, including especially depression, bipolar disorder and mania.

motivation the motive forces responsible for the initiation, persistence, direction, and vigour of goal-directed behaviour.

multiple personality disorder a rare dissociative disorder (q.v.) in which two or more markedly different personalities coexist within the same individual, popularly confused with schizophrenia (q.v.).

NA a common abbreviation for noradrenalin (q.v.).

NE a common abbreviation for norepinephrine. *See* noradrenalin.

nervous system *see under* autonomic nervous system, central nervous system (CNS), parasympathetic nervous system, sympathetic nervous system.

neurophysiology the study of the operation of the nervous system (q.v.).

neurotransmitter a chemical substance such as acetylcholine, dopamine, serotonin, or noradrenalin (qq.v.) by which a neuron (nerve cell) communicates with another neuron or with a muscle or gland.

noradrenalin one of the catecholamine (q.v.) hormones and an important neurotransmitter (q.v.) in the nervous system (q.v.), also called norepinephrine, especially in United States usage.

norepinephrine *see* noradrenalin.

out-of-body experience (OBE) *see under* depersonalization.

parapsychology from the Greek *para*, beyond + psychology, the study of psychological phenomena that appear to be paranormal (beyond the normal), notably extrasensory perception and psychokinesis (qq.v.).

parasympathetic nervous system one of the two major divisions of the autonomic nervous system; its general function is to conserve metabolic energy. *Cf.* sympathetic nervous system.

perception the processing of sensory information from the receptors (q.v.). *Cf.* sensation.

personality from the Latin *persona*, mask, the sum total of all the behavioural and mental characteristics that distinguish an individual from others.

personality disorder any of a group of mental disorders characterized by deeply ingrained, enduring, maladaptive patterns of behaviour that cause suffering to the person with the disorder or to others.

pituitary gland the master endocrine gland (q.v.), attached by a stalk to the base of the brain, which secretes into the bloodstream hormones affecting bodily growth and the functioning of other endocrine glands. *See also* adrenocorticotropic hormone (ACTH).

polygraph from the Greek *polus*, many, *graphein*, to write, an instrument for the simultaneous recording of several largely involuntary physiological responses, notably galvanic skin response (GSR) (q.v.), heart-rate, and respiration, sometimes used as a lie detector.

precognition *see under* extrasensory perception (ESP).

Prozac the proprietary name for fluoxetine hydrochloride, one of the antidepressant drugs (q.v.).

psychogalvanic response (PGR) *see* galvanic skin response (GSR).

psychokinesis from the Greek *psyche*, mind, *kinesis*, movement, in parapsychology (q.v.), the movement or change of physical objects by purely mental processes, without the application of physical forces.

psychology from the Greek *psyche*, mind, *logos*, study, the study of the nature, functions, and phenomena of behaviour and mental experience.

psychosomatic from the Greek *psyche*, mind, *soma*, body, of or relating to disorders thought to be caused or aggravated by psychological factors such as stress.

puberty from the Latin *puber*, adult, the period of development that marks the onset of adolescence when secondary sexual characteristics emerge.

receptor a sense organ or structure that is sensitive to a specific form of physical energy and that transmits neural information to other parts of the nervous system.

retrograde amnesia *see* amnesia.

schizophrenia from the Greek *schizein*, to split, *phren*, mind, a group of mental disorders characterized by incoherent thought and speech, hallucinations (q.v.), delusions (q.v.), flattened or inappropriate affect, deterioration of social functioning, and lack of self care. In spite of its derivation, the word does not refer to multiple personality disorder (q.v.).

sensation acquisition by the body's internal and external sense organs or receptors (q.v.) of 'raw' information. *Cf.* perception.

sensory memory a form of memory, necessary for normal vision and hearing, which allows visual images to be stored for about half a second and sounds for up to two seconds. Sensory memory enables television, which presents 30 still images per second, to convey the illusion of a single moving image. It also makes speech intelligible, because without it, by the end of each spoken word the hearer would have forgotten its beginning. *Cf.* long-term memory, short-term memory.

short-term memory (STM) a memory store, also called working memory, consisting of a central executive, visuo-spatial sketchpad, and articulatory loop that is used for storing small amounts of information for periods of time ranging from a few seconds to a few minutes. It has a severely limited capacity of about seven or eight items of information, such as digits of a telephone number, and the information is rapidly forgotten unless it is refreshed by rehearsal, following which it may eventually be transferred to long-term memory (LTM) (q.v.).

serotonin one of the neurotransmitter (q.v.) substances in the nervous system, also known as 5-hydroxytryptamine or 5-HT.

stereotype from the Greek *stereos*, solid, *tupos*, type, an over-simplified, biased, and above all inflexible conception of a social group. The word was originally used in the printing trade for a solid metallic plate which was difficult to alter once cast.

stimulants hormones such as adrenalin, noradrenalin, and dopamine (qq.v.), and drugs such as amphetamines, that increase physiological arousal in general and central nervous system (q.v.) activity in particular.

stressor any stimulus, event or state of affairs that causes stress.

subjects from the Latin *sub*, under, *jacere*, to throw, people or other organisms whose behaviour or mental experience is investigated in psychological research.

sympathetic nervous system one of the two major divisions of the autonomic nervous system; it is concerned with general activation, and it mobilizes the body's reaction to stress or perceived danger. *Cf.* parasympathetic nervous system.

telepathy *see under* extrasensory perception (ESP).

trance logic, hypnotic a peculiar willingness of many hypnotic subjects to tolerate logical inconsistencies without apparent discomfort (for example, to see a hallucination of a person and the actual person at different places in the same room) in contrast to subjects trying to simulate hypnosis, who usually eliminate the inconsistencies.

tricyclic antidepressants *see* antidepressant drugs.

Type A behaviour pattern a personality type, possibly associated with an increased risk of coronary heart disease, characterized by an exaggerated sense of urgency, competitiveness, ambition, and hostile aggressiveness when thwarted.

weapon focus a phenomenon in forensic (crimonological) psychology (q.v.) whereby eyewitnesses to incidents involving firearms or other dangerous weapons tend to concentrate on the weapon and fail to notice or remember other details of the incident.

Yerkes-Dodson law a psychological law named after its proposers stating that optimal performance on a variety of tasks occurs at intermediate levels of arousal (q.v.).

INDEX